ZEN COLORING PAGES FOR ADULTS

Table Of Contents:

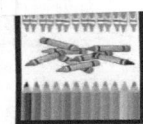

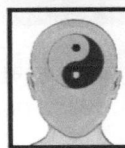

Author's Note: This book is designed for both right-handers and left-handers to enjoy with ease!

Common Questions & Answers:

I'm an adult! Why would I need to color like a little kid?

Because as an adult, you need play-time more than ever. Think about all the stress and worry in your life. Wouldn't a little whimsy for a few minutes a day make a huge impact on you? With this book, you get 30 full pages of stress relief – in the palm of your hands!

Besides stress relief and personal growth, what "other good" comes from this book?

Great question – and I'm glad you asked. Thirty percent (30%) of the profits from every book sold will go to TNR (Trap-Neuter-Release) programs to help reduce the stray cat population in Florida … because cats are cool and so are you!

I have no plans to get rich off these pages. My best hope is to help some kitt-ehs, and to spread the love. Helping you be the very best YOU that you can be by becoming more Zen – is my primary goal. Positive thoughts, my friends!

ZEN COLORING PAGES: ME-ZANGLES

What Are *Me-Zangles*?

Me-Zangles (mee zanglz) are one type of pre-designed pages to which you add your own structured patterns to craft unique and uplifting artistic creations. They are based on the *Zentangle Method*, which is described below.

The *Zentangle Method*:

According to their website www.zentangle.com, "The *Zentangle Method* is an easy-to-learn, relaxing, and fun way to create beautiful images by drawing structured patterns …. We believe that life is an art form and that our *Zentangle Method* is an elegant metaphor for deliberate artistry in life."

Finding the *Zentangle Method* website was a moment of epiphany for me, as I have been drawing these for more than twenty years – since I saw my first college roommate doing it. I never knew there was a specific philosophy around the technique – and was so glad to learn it that I had to share it with you! I have found the practice so stimulating-yet-relaxing that my own *Me-Zangles* have decorated everything from my classwork to work meeting notes to pages in my journals.

By teaching yourself this method, you are gaining a life-long outlet for your creativity that develops you – personally - in a variety of ways. We'll get more into the true benefits of these coloring pages soon.

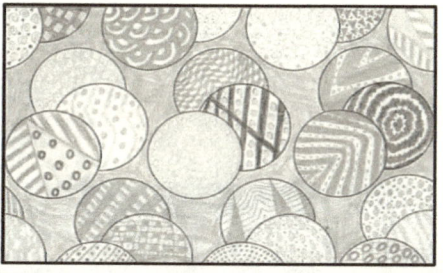 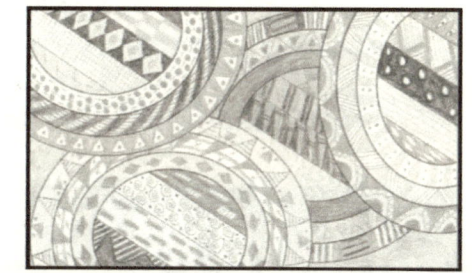

What Are *Zen Shapes*?

Zen Shapes are one type of pre-designed pages to which you add your own structured patterns to craft unique and uplifting artistic creations. They are based off common shapes and forms, and each page is set up with a cohesive synthesis of shapes in creating a unique whole – for you to make even more unique!

There are three basic types of forms used to create the *Zen Shapes* pages:

- ❖ **Geometric:** These include squares, triangles, and circles, as examples, and most often are stylistically symmetrical and structured. They add dimension and a sense of equality to the pages.

- ❖ **Abstract:** These are typically outlines of common forms or shapes, but generally lack true formation, like a spiral, for example. There is an innate sense of movement and harmony built into these free-flowing shapes.

- ❖ **Organic:** These most often represent something from the natural world, like clouds or stars, lending visual coherence and commonality to the pages.

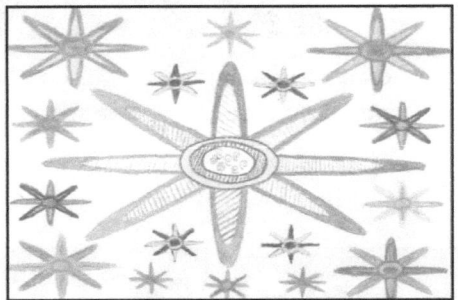

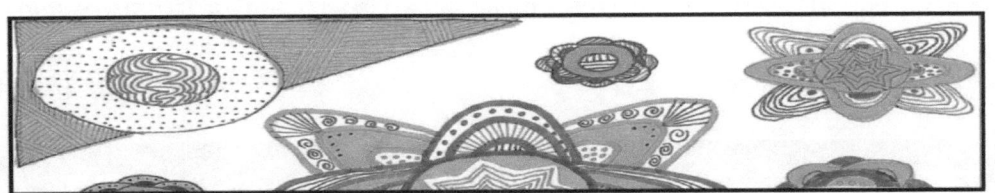

ZEN COLORING PAGES: WORDLES

What Are *Wordles*?

Wordles (werd lz) are one type of pre-designed word clouds to which you add your own structured patterns to craft unique and uplifting artistic creations. They are based on the word clouds created on the *Wordle* website, which is described below.

Wordles:

According to their website www.wordle.net, "*Wordle* is a toy for generating 'word clouds' from text that you provide. The clouds give greater prominence to words that appear more frequently in the source text."

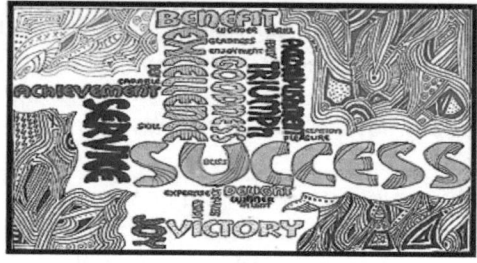 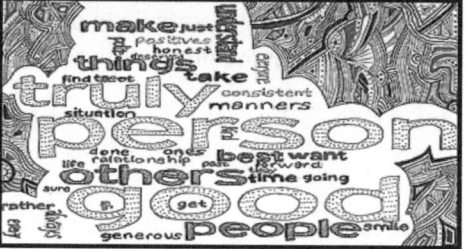

For the *Wordles* included in this book, I searched for articles featuring the "base words" I wanted to highlight in my word clouds – those on which you, the artist, can focus your energy and attention. I have always loved and respected words – and the power behind them – and hope that, in coloring these word clouds, you let these particular words melt deep into your soul. Positive thoughts, my friends!

Read about the benefits of *Zen Coloring Pages* next!

Benefits Gained Using *Zen Coloring Pages for Adults:*

- **Increased Problem-Solving Skills:** Discovering new and different ways to complete each section inspires you to greater and greater depths of creative and critical thought. Sometimes, in coloring these pages, you may feel a stroke committed to the page is an error. Instead, view this "mistake" not as an error, but as a new direction that can lead to an entirely new pattern within the drawing – and go with it!

- **Improved Concentration & Focus:** Completing one of the *Zen Coloring Pages* takes very specific focus and effort. The dedication needed for this task lets you entangle your mind in the creation process – thus allowing in fresh perspectives through a relaxed and creative flow.

- **Improved Anger Management / Increased Positive Behaviors:** Those who are often angry will especially find solace in the *Zen Coloring Pages*. The technique requires that nearly all thought is focused solely on completing the task – which allows you to more easily let go of the anger while channeling it in a healthy direction.

- **Increased Relaxation & Stress Relief / Increased Inner Balance & Peace:** Once you have completed one of the *Zen Coloring Pages*, you will understand the peaceful mindset that occurs when you are creating them. All people, but especially those who experience higher levels of anxiety or external stress and chaos, will find comfort and stress relief in the creation process.

- **Increased Self-Empowerment:** Each of the *Zen Coloring Pages* page offers a collection of limits (through specific borders within which to draw), which serve as mini-goals to be reached. As you complete each section of a page, your confidence in "being creative" will grow – thus empowering you to continue!

Your Primary Goal:

Finish as many as you can in one year's time. Enjoy the journey, my friends!

ZEN COLORING PAGES: MORE BENEFITS

More Benefits Gained Using *Zen Coloring Pages for Adults:*

- **Improved Self-Esteem:** In completing one of the *Zen Coloring Pages*, you are able to see that, with time, focus, and effort, a complicated and intricate finished piece can be developed – one line at a time. This transfers to a sense that anything (no matter how difficult) can be accomplished – with the proper time, focus, and effort.

- **Increased Mindfulness:** Each stroke you make is conscious and deliberate – and helps you clearly see how many small-yet-significant details make up a beautiful holistic image.

- **Increased Creativity & Individuality:** *Zen Coloring Pages* are especially wonderful for those who feel they are "not creative". Through the simple repetition of adding colors, shapes, angles, and lines, any person can become a creative artist in a very short time! Once "non-creative" people have experienced initial creative success, their energy for more individual and unique creation grows exponentially! Also, since each person creating the *Zen Coloring Pages* is unique – it is a celebration of pure self-expression and encourages individuality!

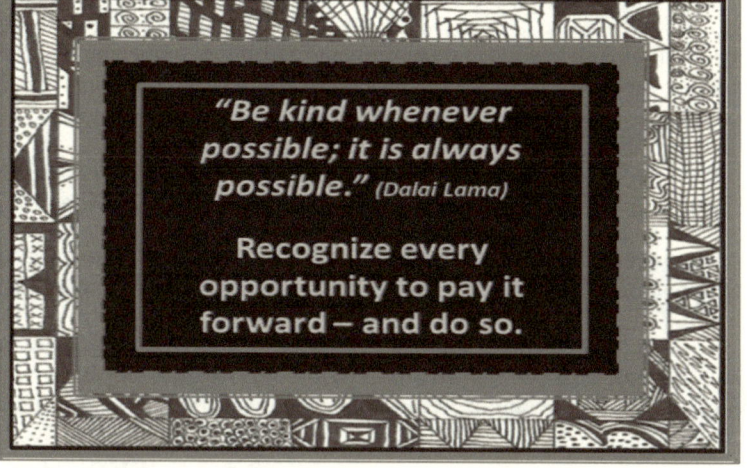

"Be kind whenever possible; it is always possible." (Dalai Lama)

Recognize every opportunity to pay it forward – and do so.

Author's Note: I hope you enjoy the journey to becoming more Zen as much as I've enjoyed creating these pages to help you focus on that journey! Positive thoughts, my friends!

ZEN COLORING PAGES FOR ADULTS

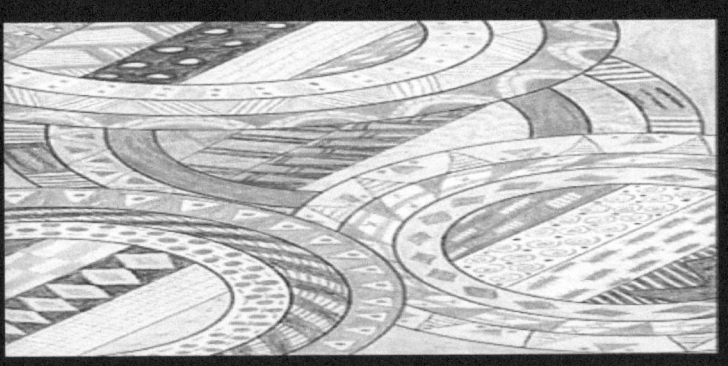
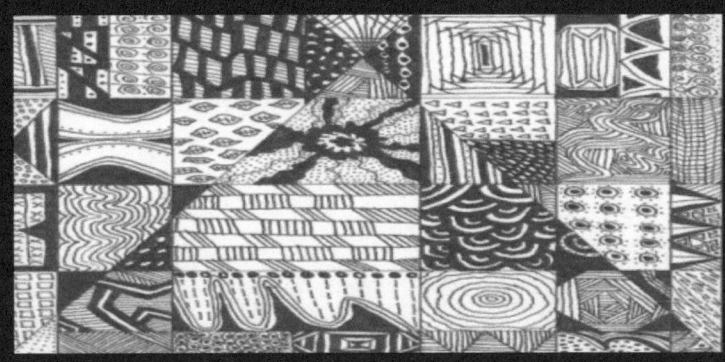

ME-ZANGLES

ME-ZANGLES #1

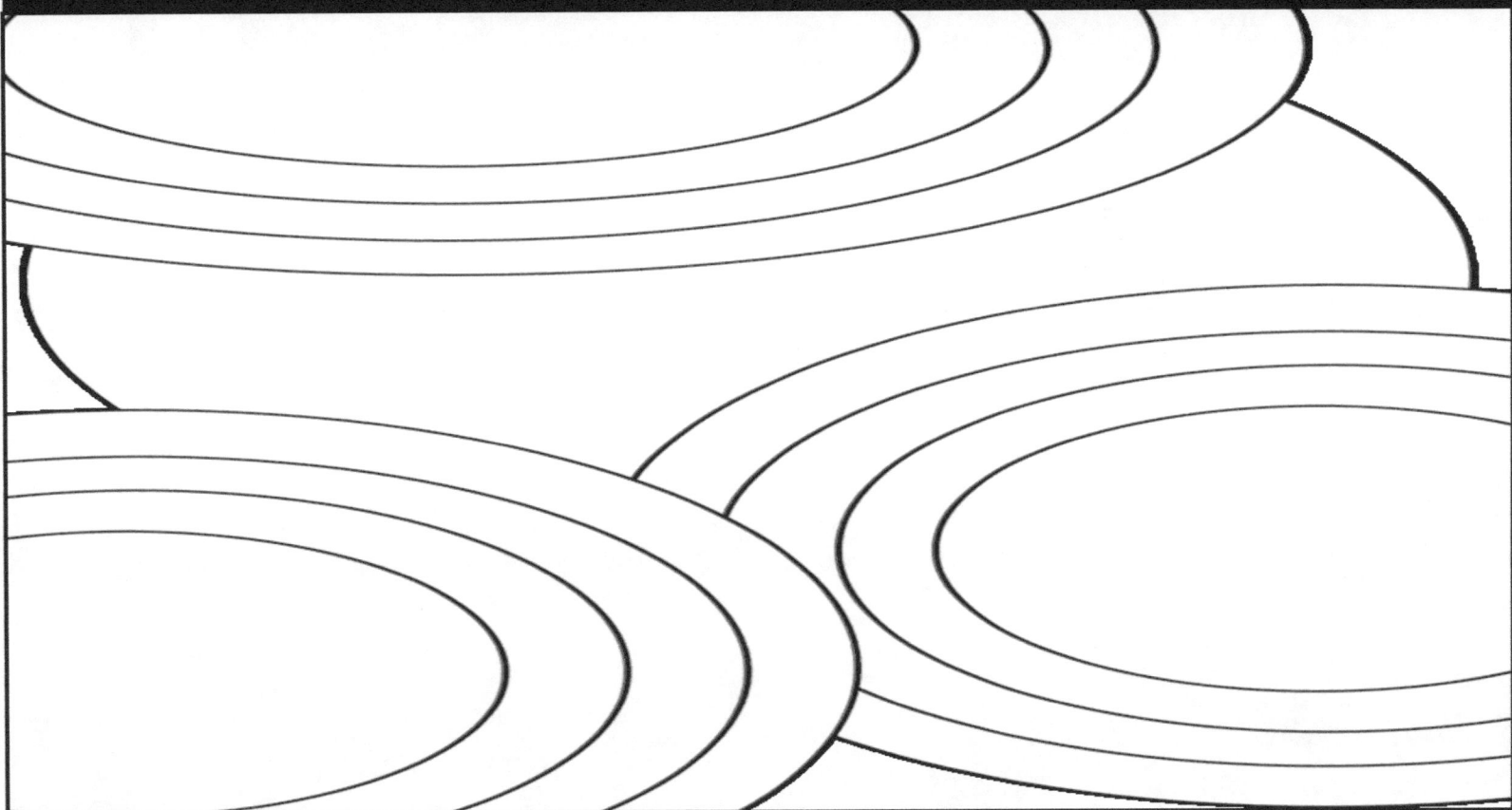

ME-ZANGLES #2

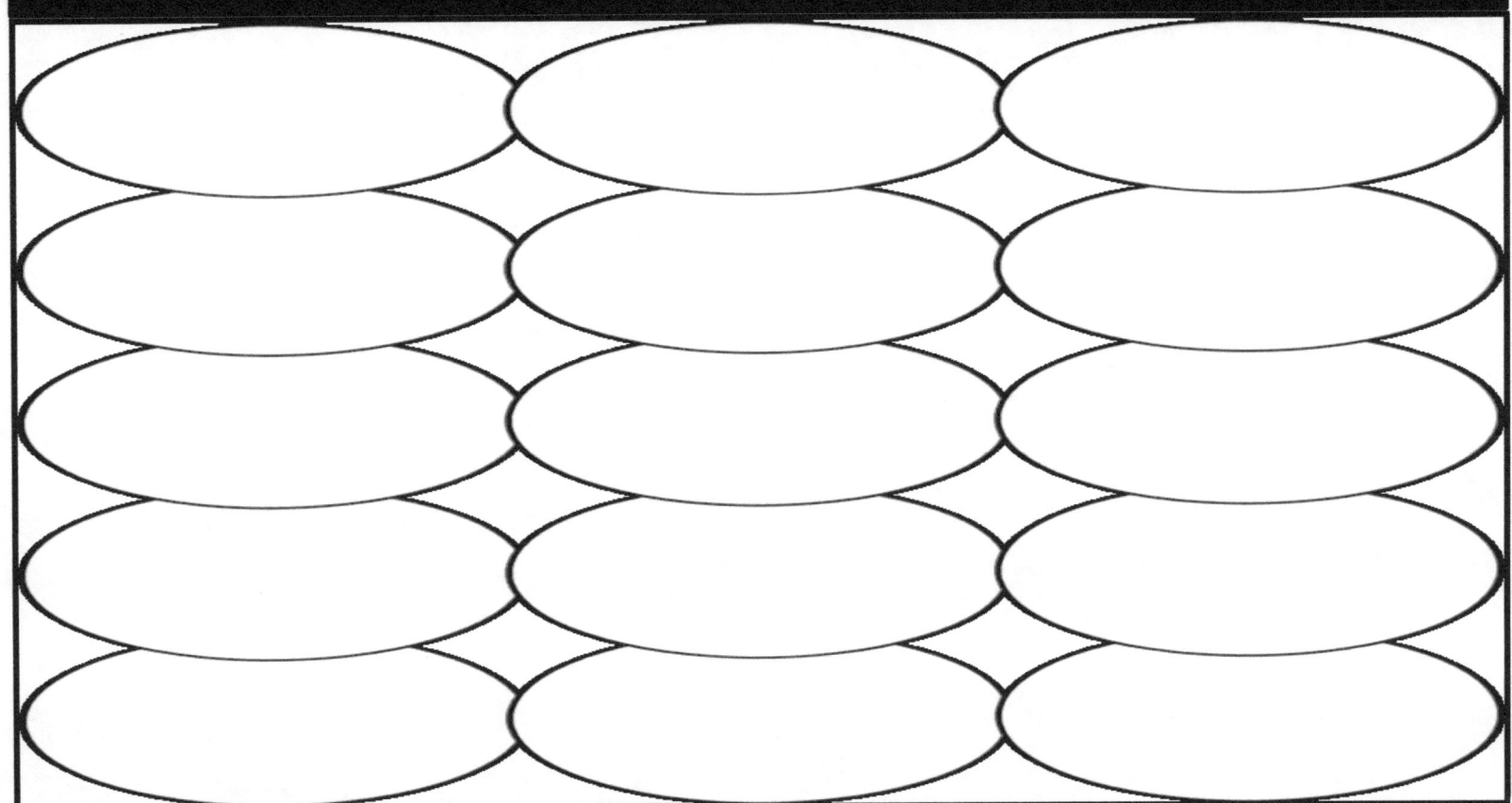

ME-ZANGLES #3

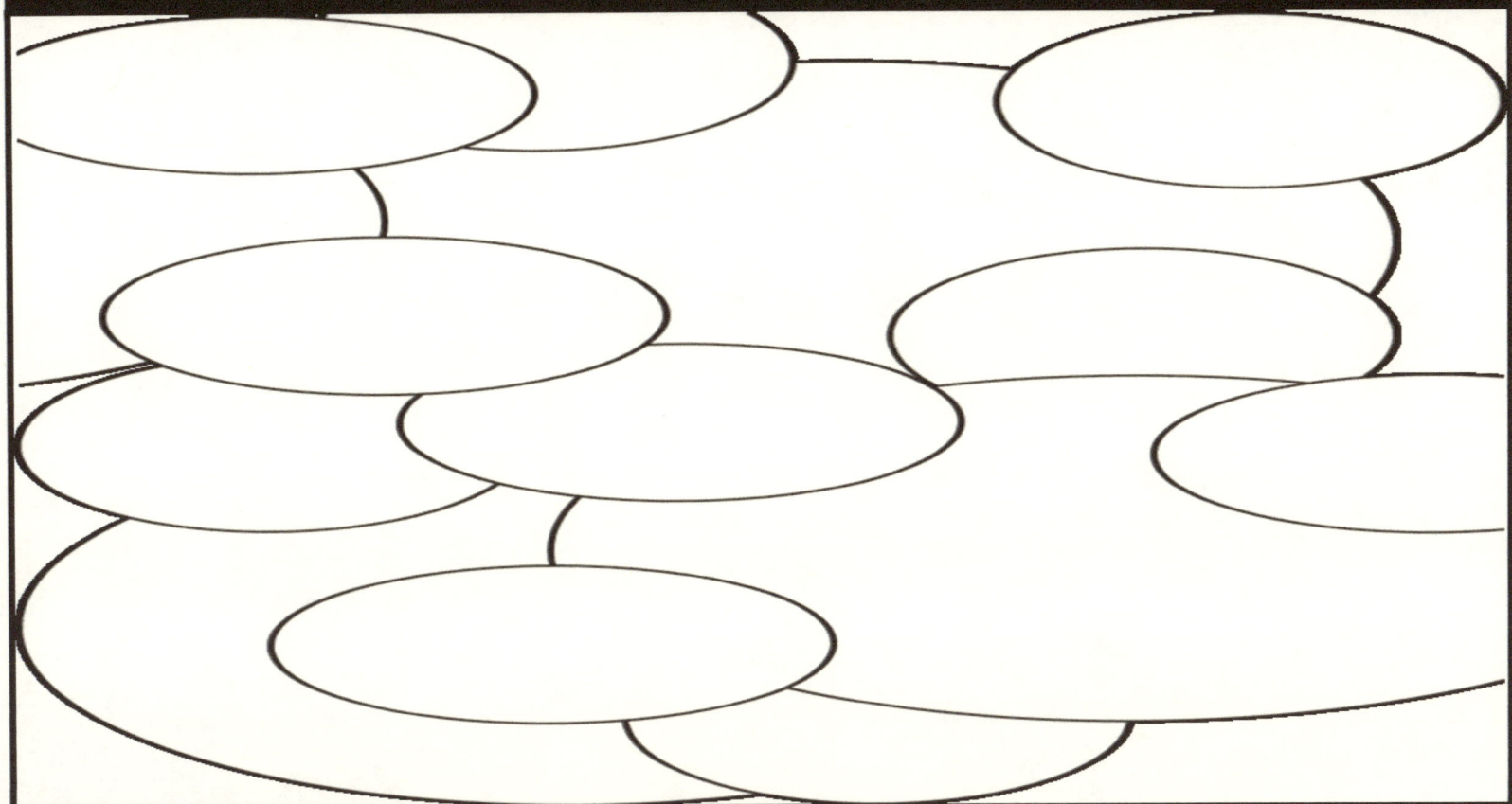

ME-ZANGLES #4

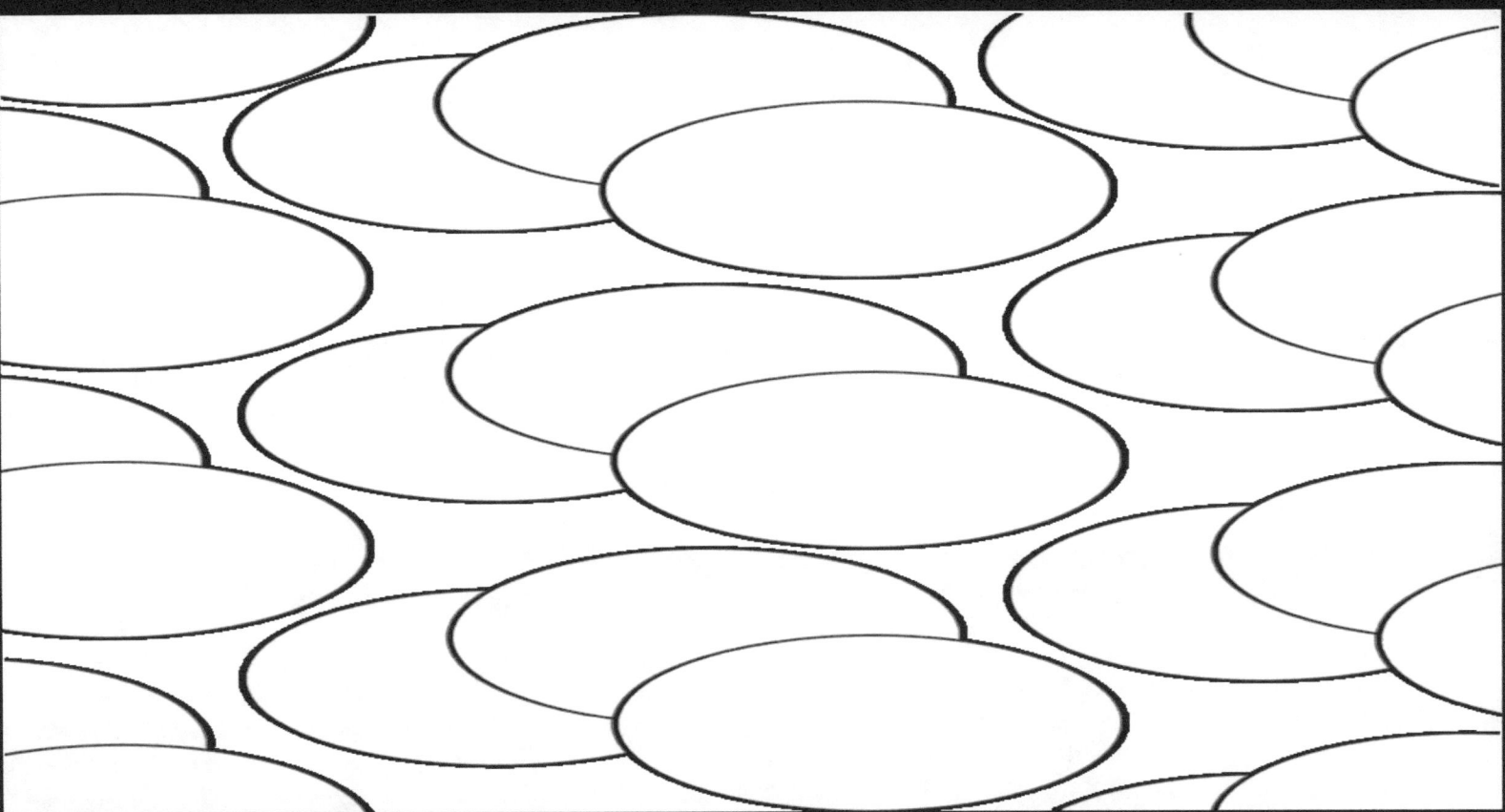

ME-ZANGLES #5

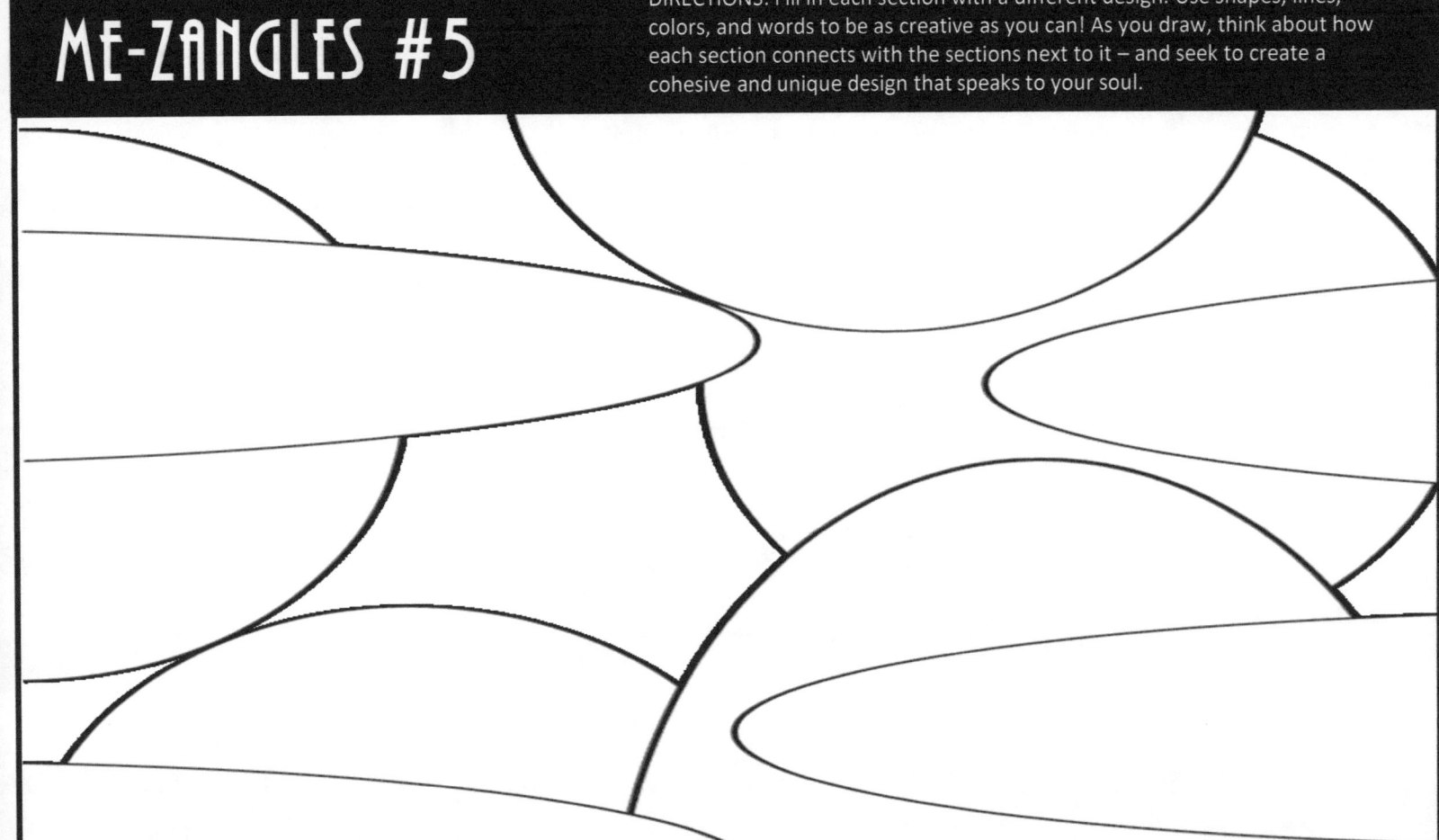

DIRECTIONS: Fill in each section with a different design. Use shapes, lines, colors, and words to be as creative as you can! As you draw, think about how each section connects with the sections next to it – and seek to create a cohesive and unique design that speaks to your soul.

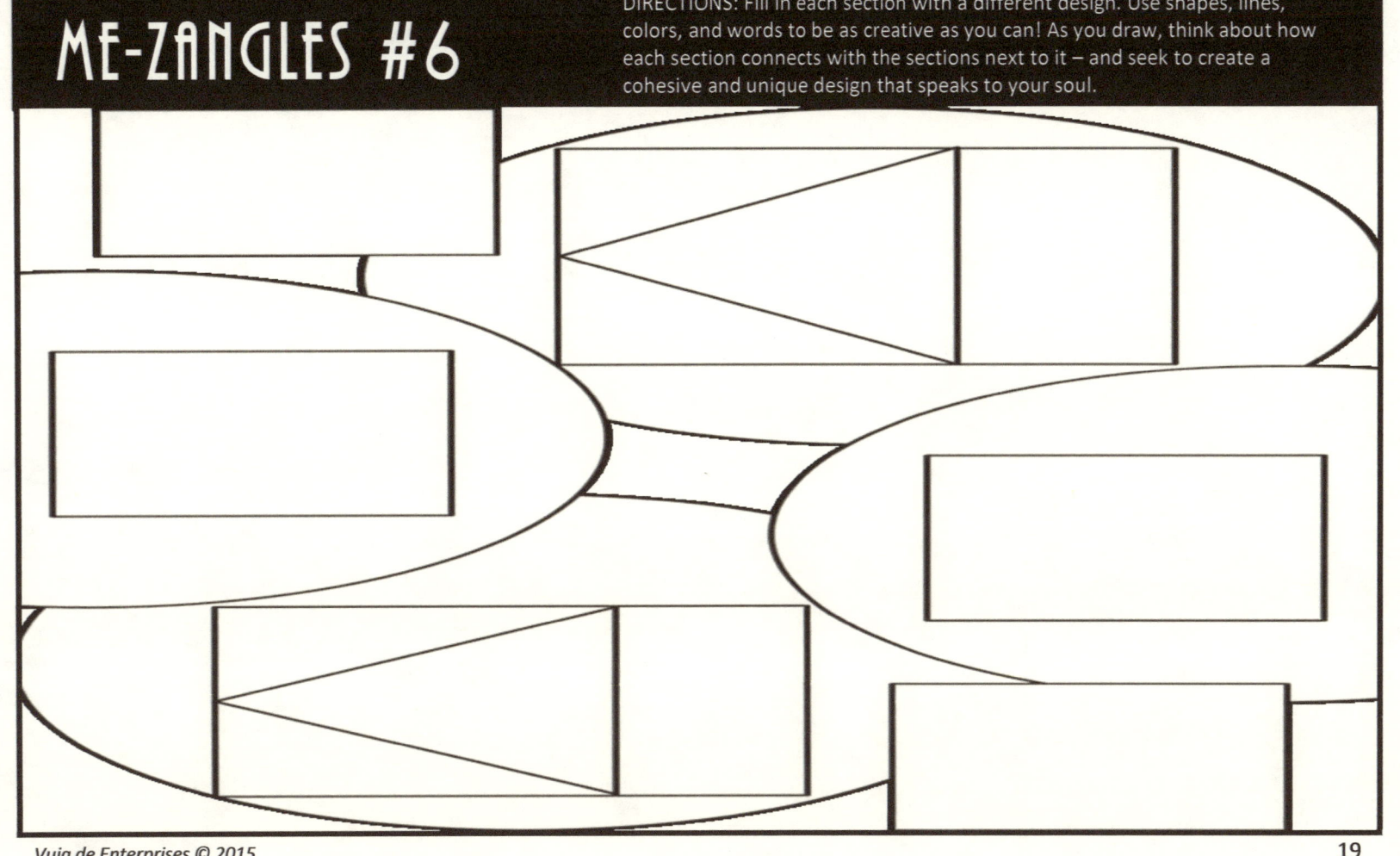

DIRECTIONS: Fill in each section with a different design. Use shapes, lines, colors, and words to be as creative as you can! As you draw, think about how each section connects with the sections next to it – and seek to create a cohesive and unique design that speaks to your soul.

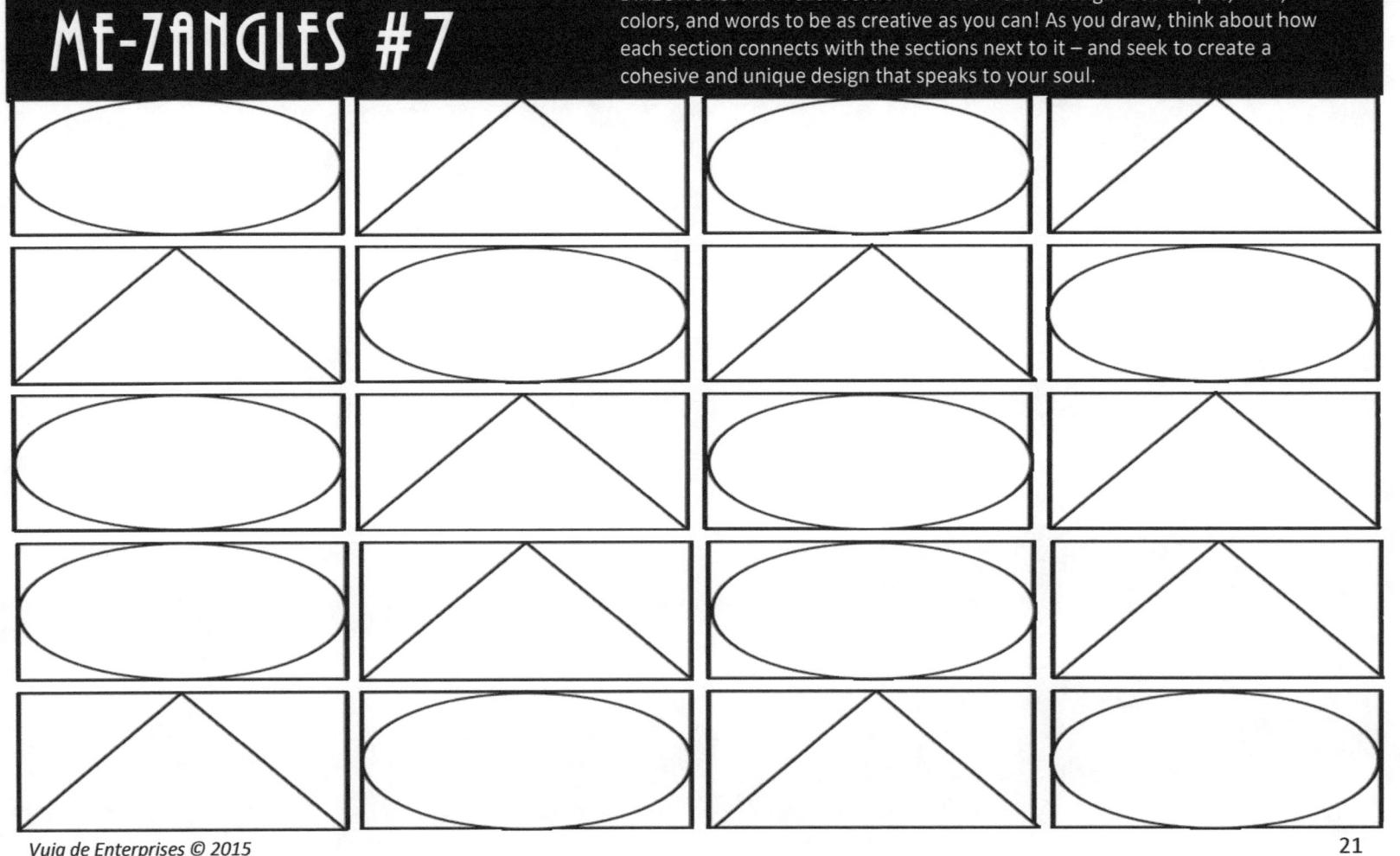

ME-ZANGLES #8

ME-ZANGLES #9

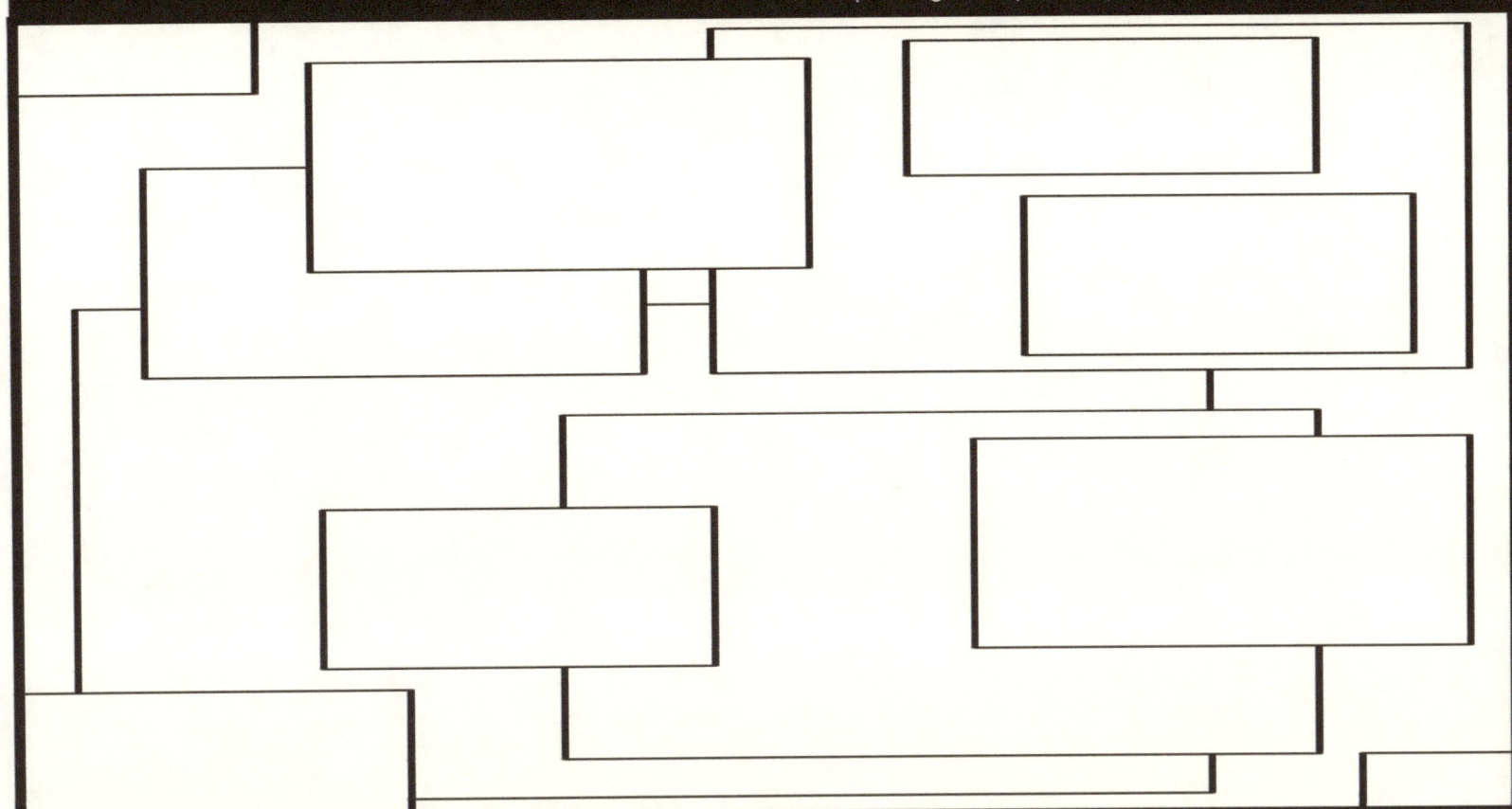

ME-ZANGLES #10

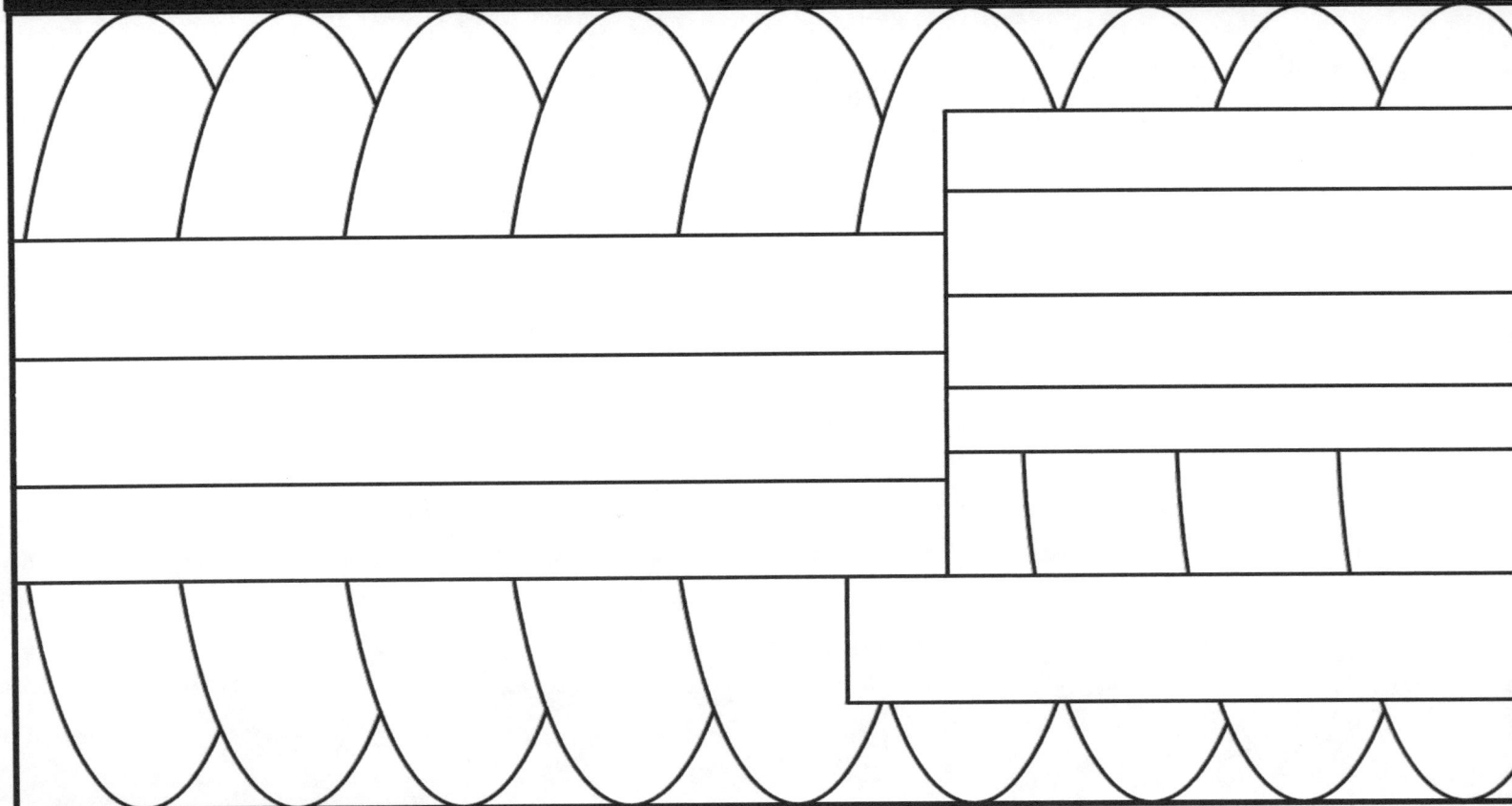

ME-ZANGLES #11

Vuja de Enterprises © 2015

ME-ZANGLES #12

ME-ZANGLES #13

DIRECTIONS: Fill in each section with a different design. Use shapes, lines, colors, and words to be as creative as you can! As you draw, think about how each section connects with the sections next to it – and seek to create a cohesive and unique design that speaks to your soul.

ME-ZANGLES #14

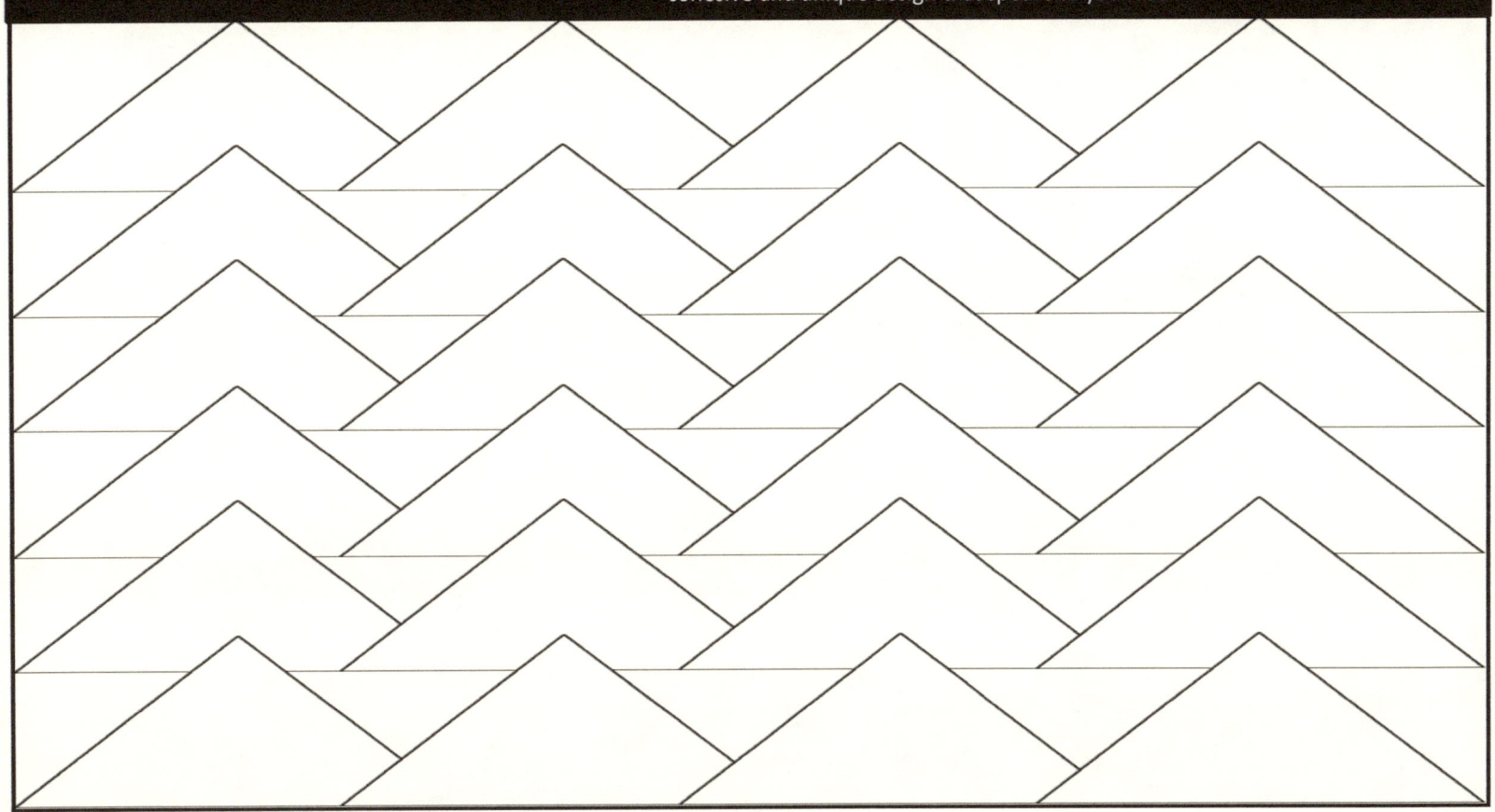

Vuja de Enterprises © 2015

ME-ZANGLES #15

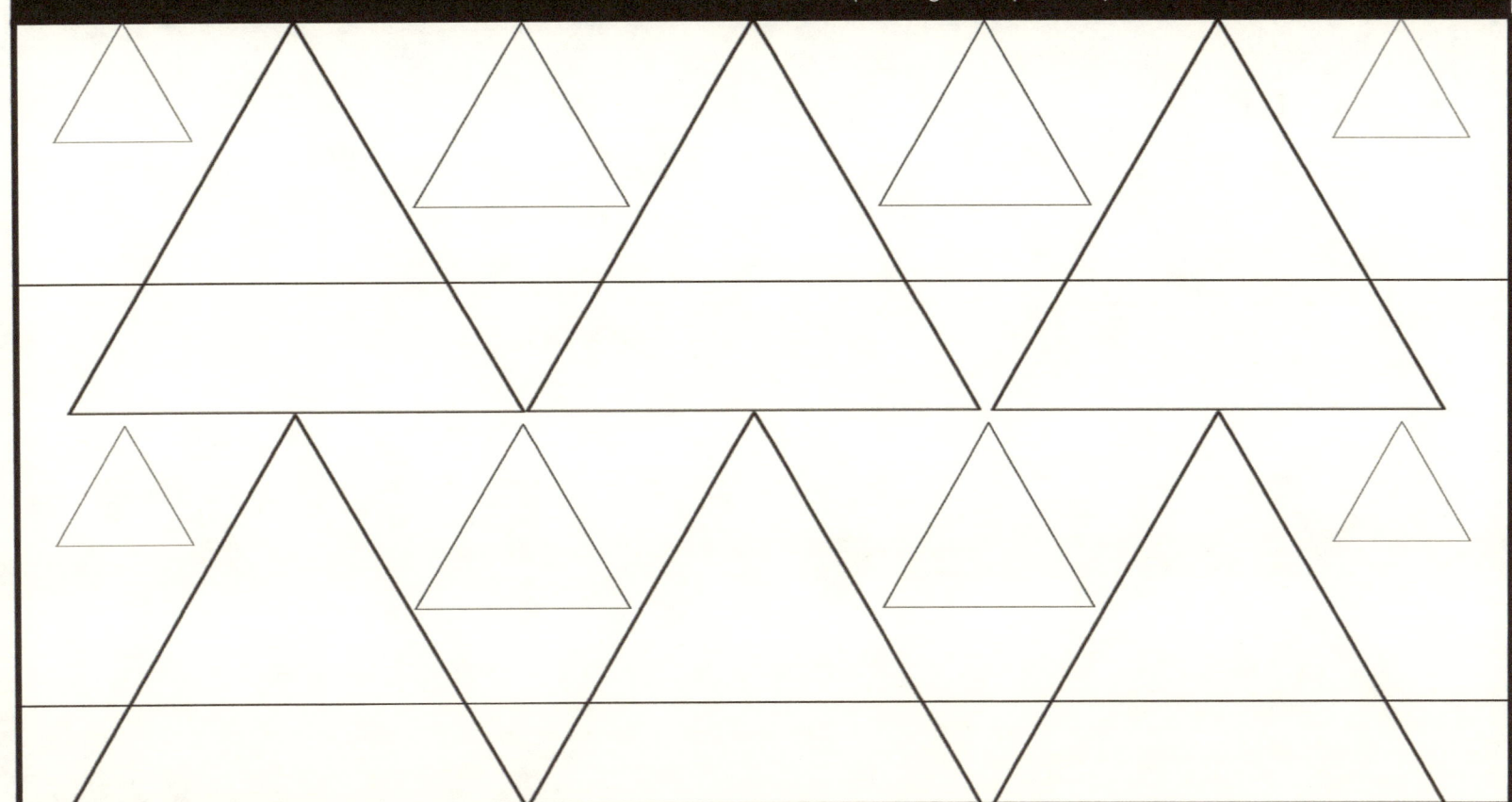

Vuja de Enterprises © 2015

ZEN COLORING PAGES FOR ADULTS

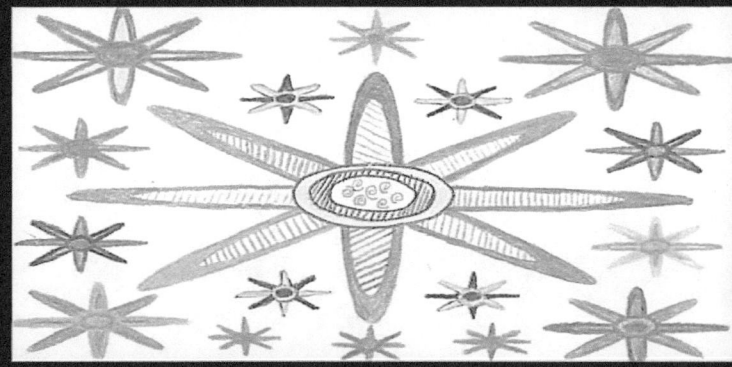

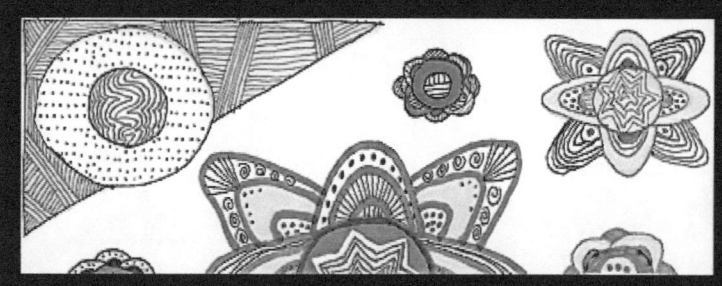

ZEN SHAPES

ZEN SHAPES #1

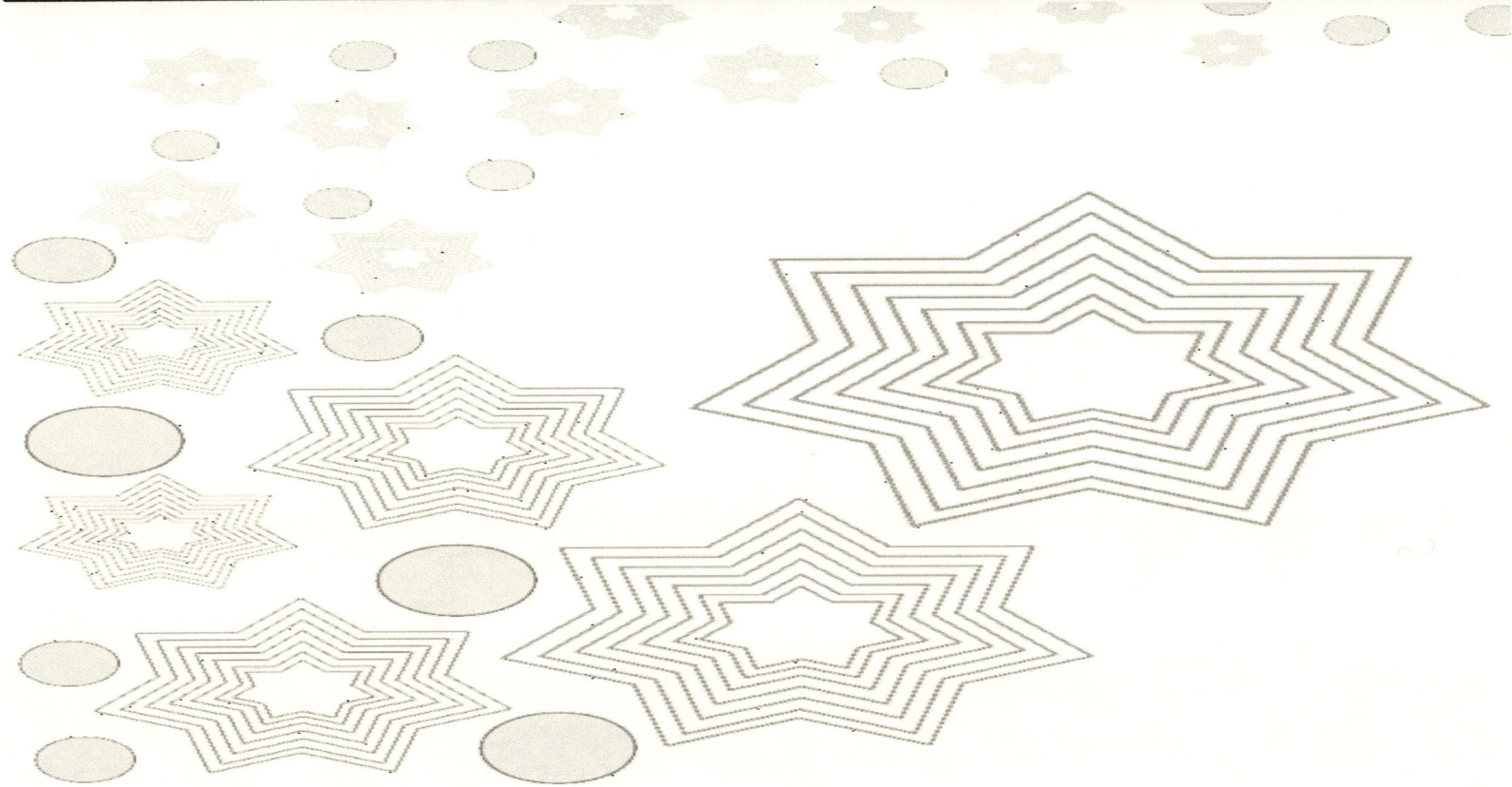

ZEN SHAPES #2

DIRECTIONS: Fill in each shape with a different design. Use shapes, lines, colors, and words to be as creative as you can! As you draw, think about how each shape connects with the shapes next to it – and seek to create a cohesive and unique design that speaks to your soul.

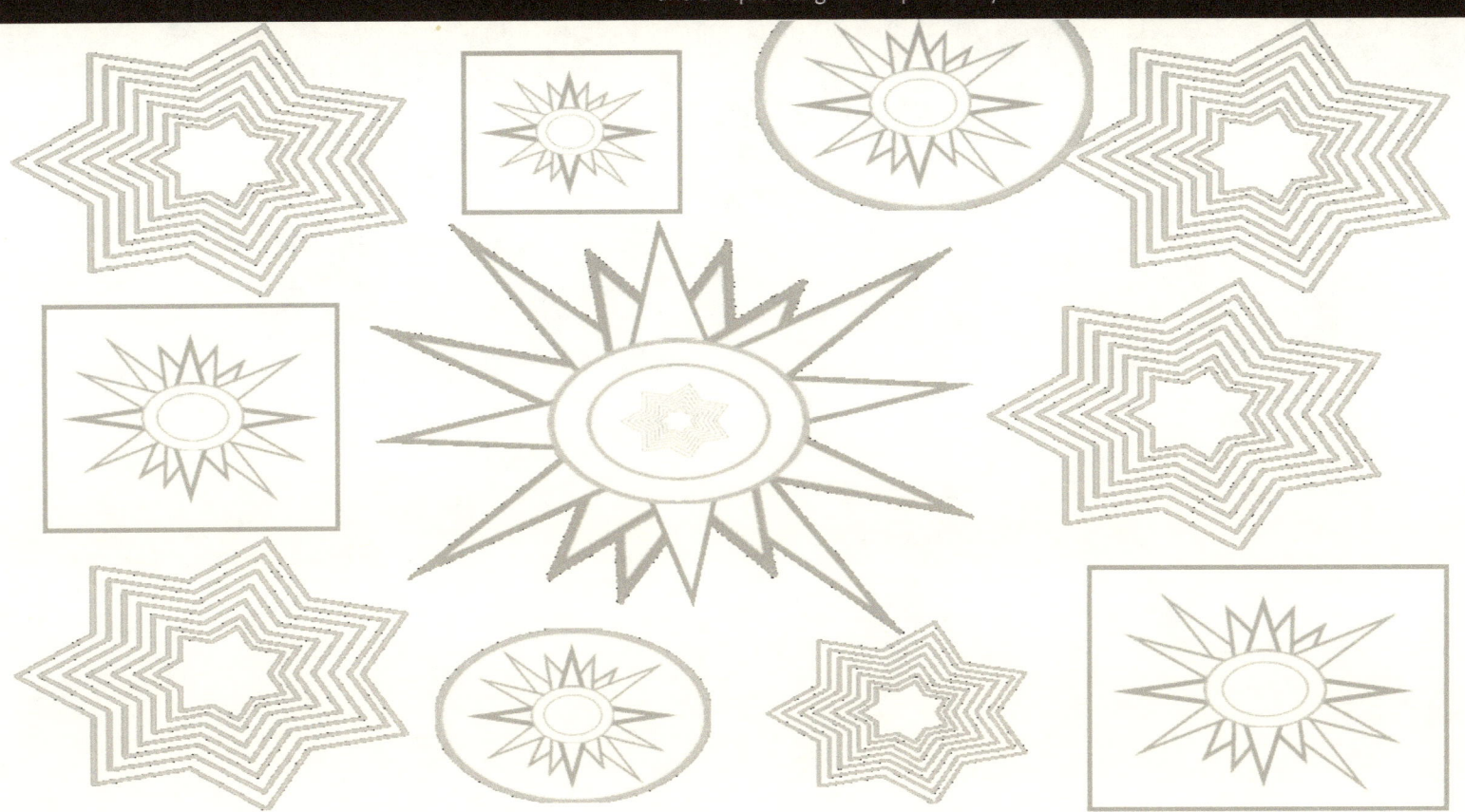

ZEN SHAPES #3

DIRECTIONS: Fill in each shape with a different design. Use shapes, lines, colors, and words to be as creative as you can! As you draw, think about how each shape connects with the shapes next to it – and seek to create a cohesive and unique design that speaks to your soul.

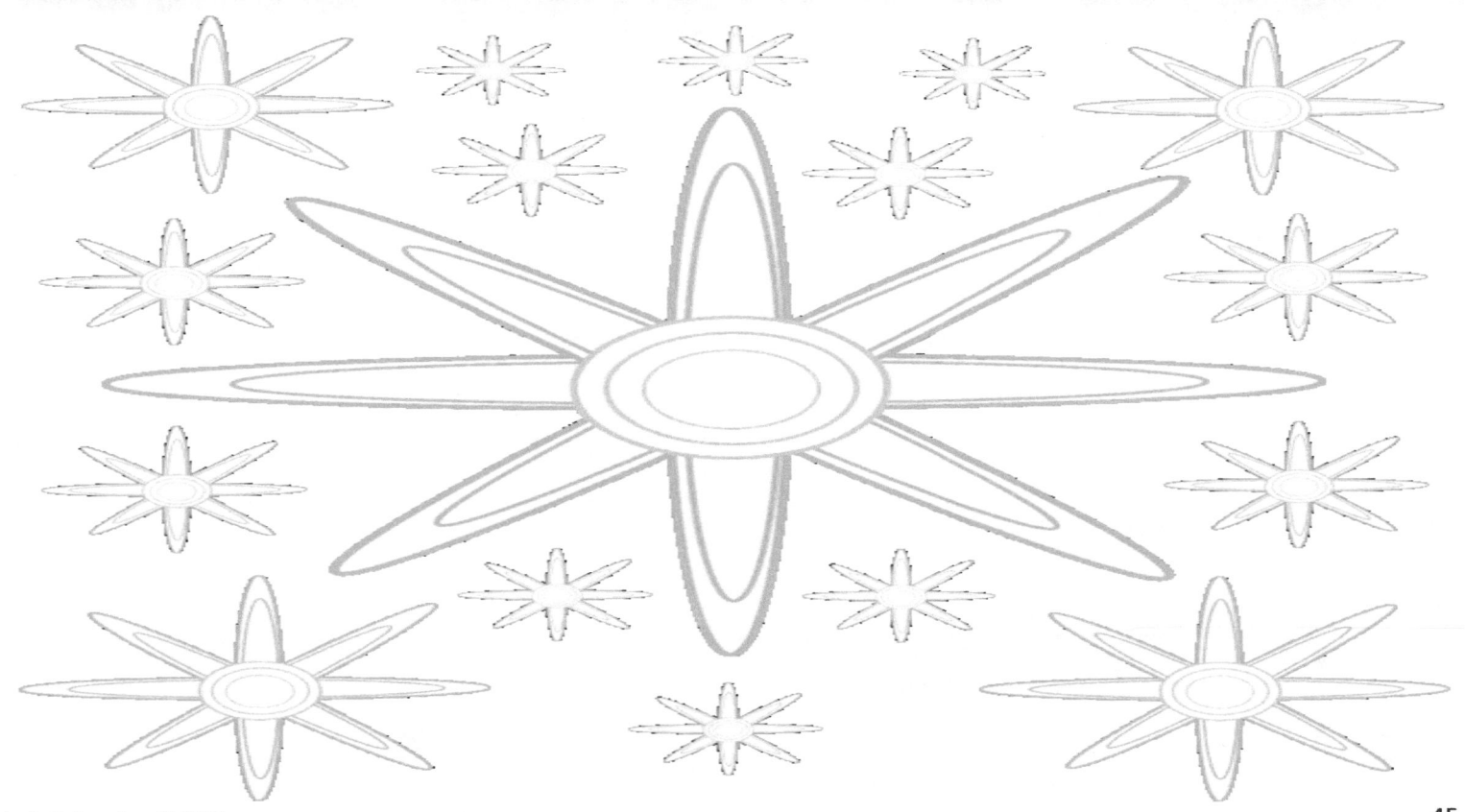

ZEN SHAPES #4

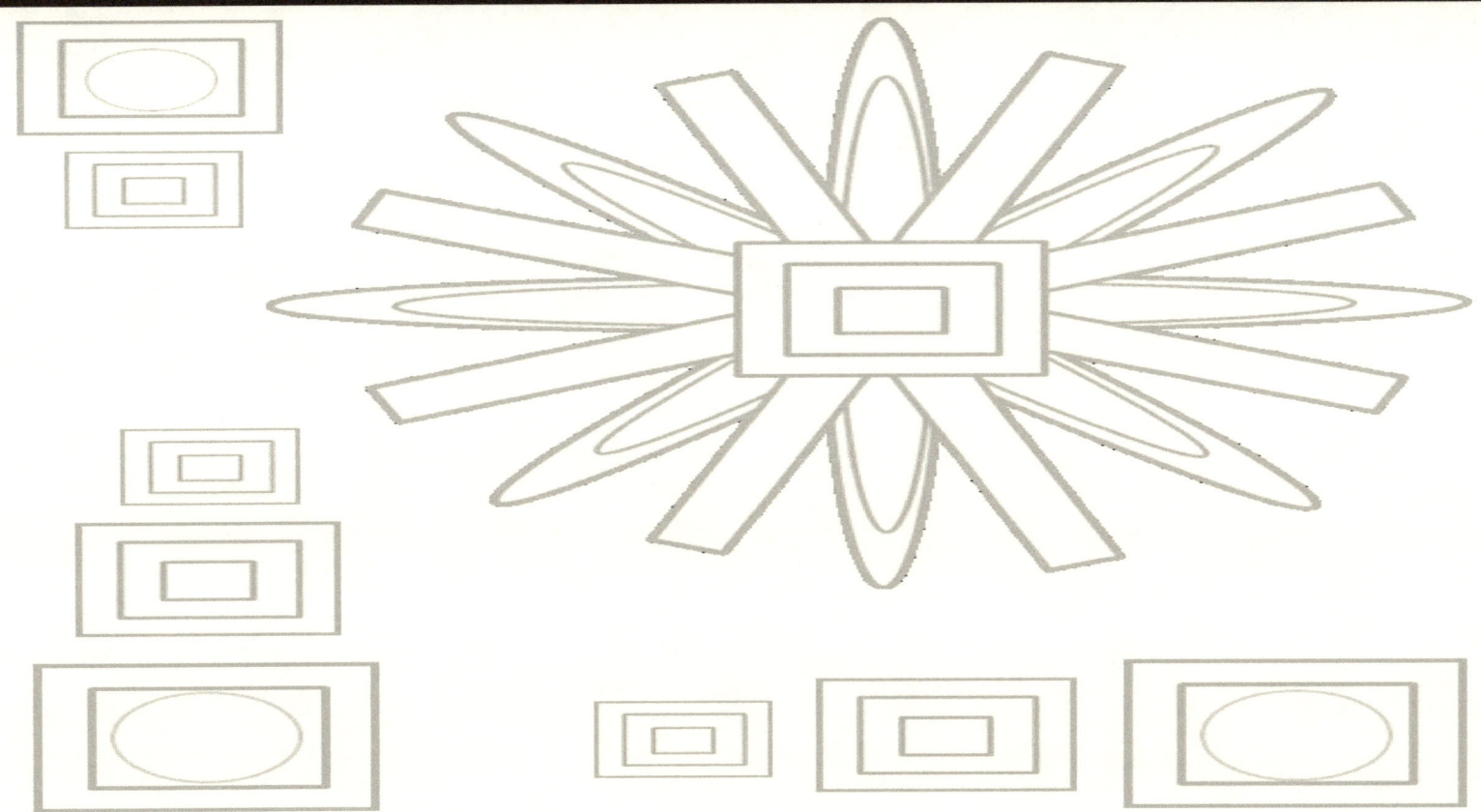

ZEN SHAPES #5

DIRECTIONS: Fill in each shape with a different design. Use shapes, lines, colors, and words to be as creative as you can! As you draw, think about how each shape connects with the shapes next to it – and seek to create a cohesive and unique design that speaks to your soul.

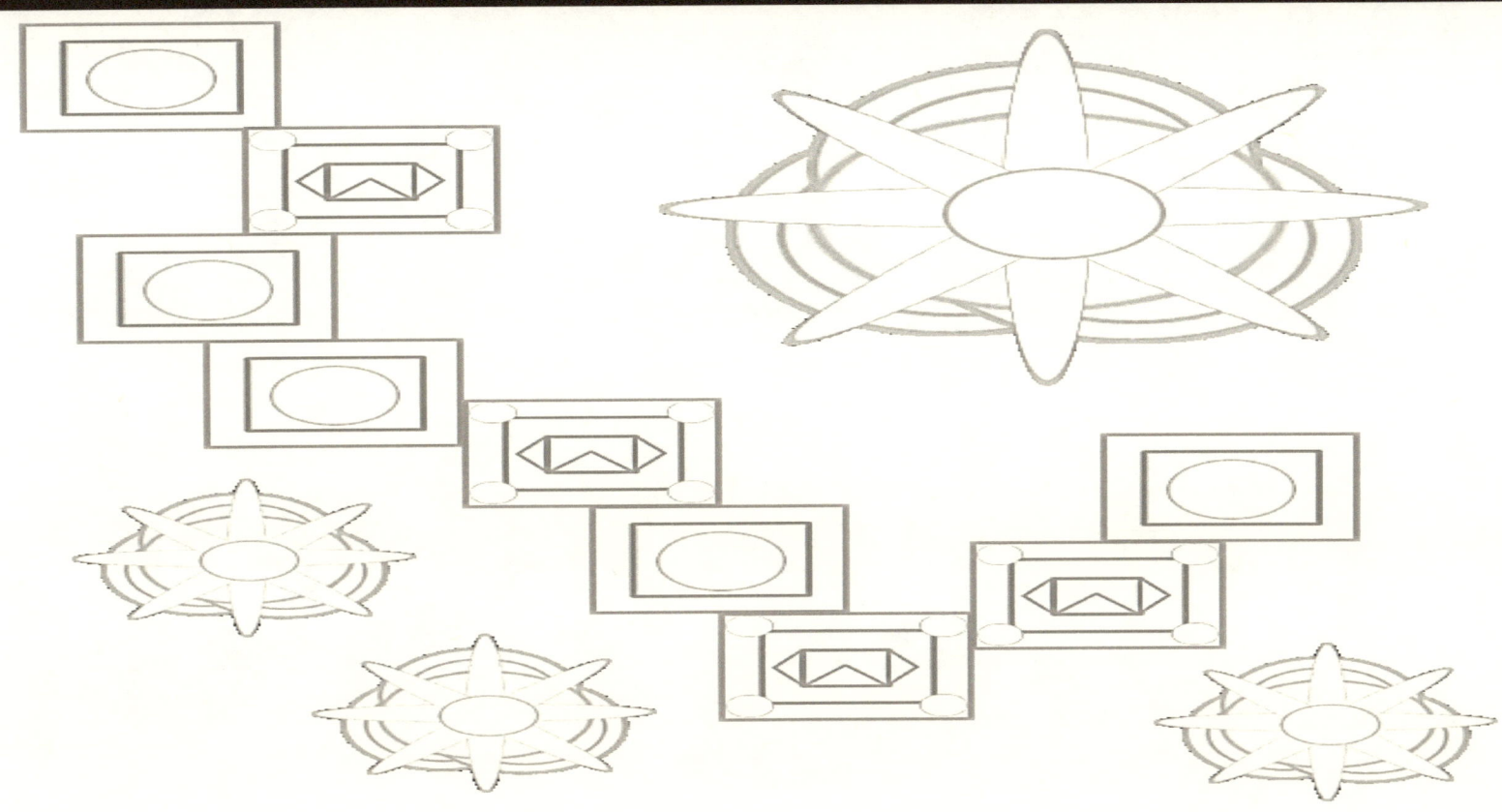

DIRECTIONS: Fill in each shape with a diffe̶rent design. Use shapes, lines, colors, and words to be as creative as you can! As you draw, think about how each shape connects with the shapes next to it – and seek to create a cohesive and unique design that speaks to your soul.

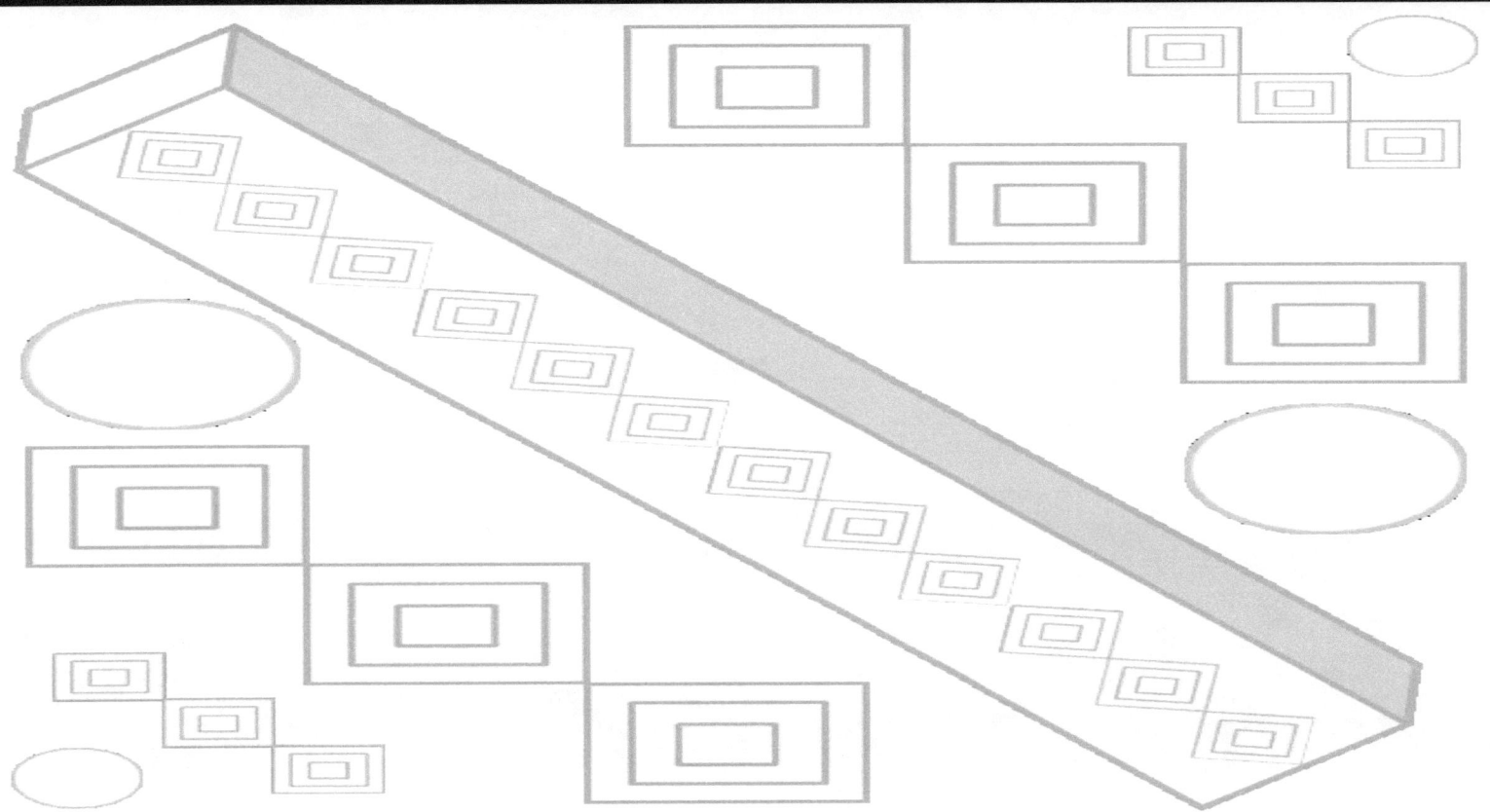

DIRECTIONS: Fill in each shape with a different design, shapes, lines, colors, and words to be as creative as you can! As you draw, think about how each shape connects with the shapes next to it – and seek to create a cohesive and unique design that speaks to your soul.

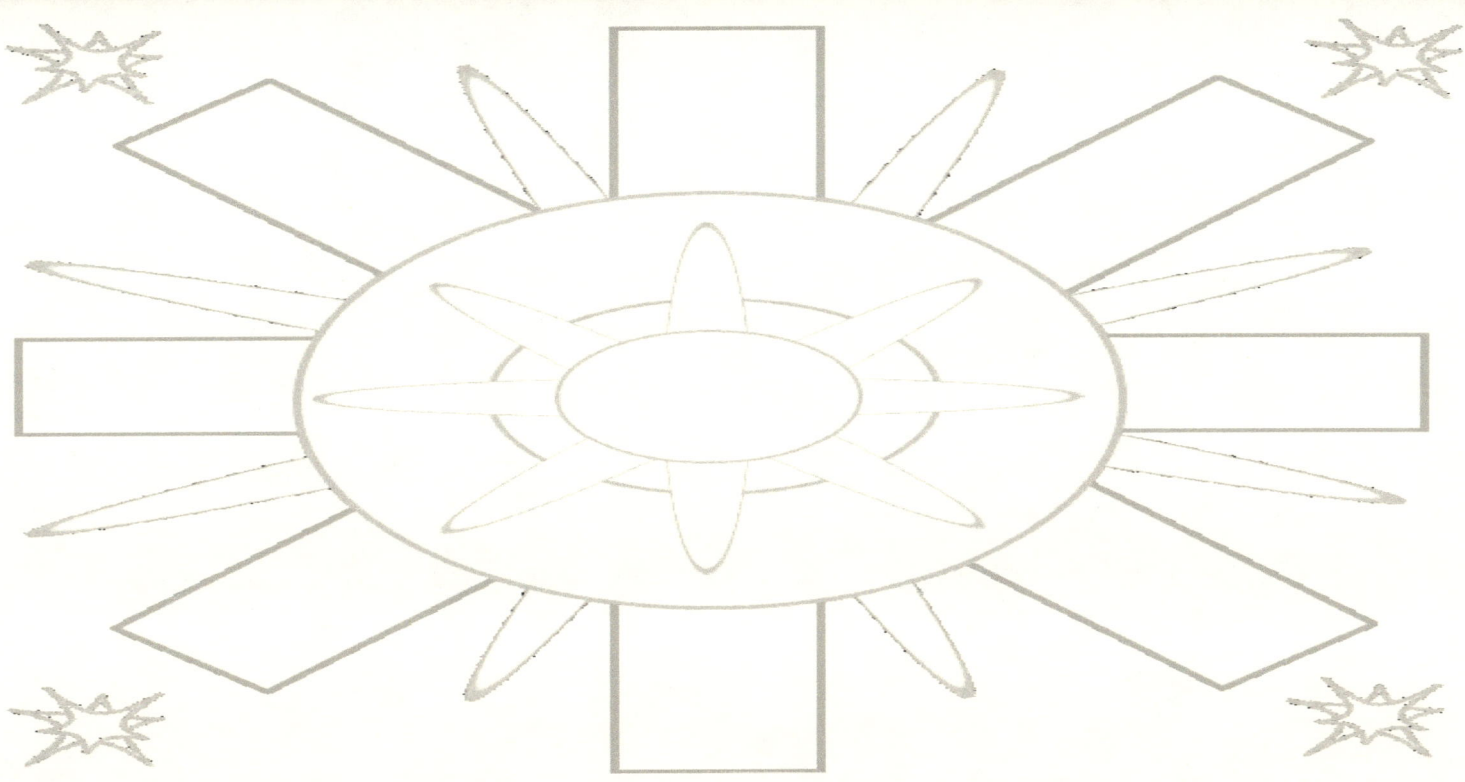

ZEN SHAPES #8

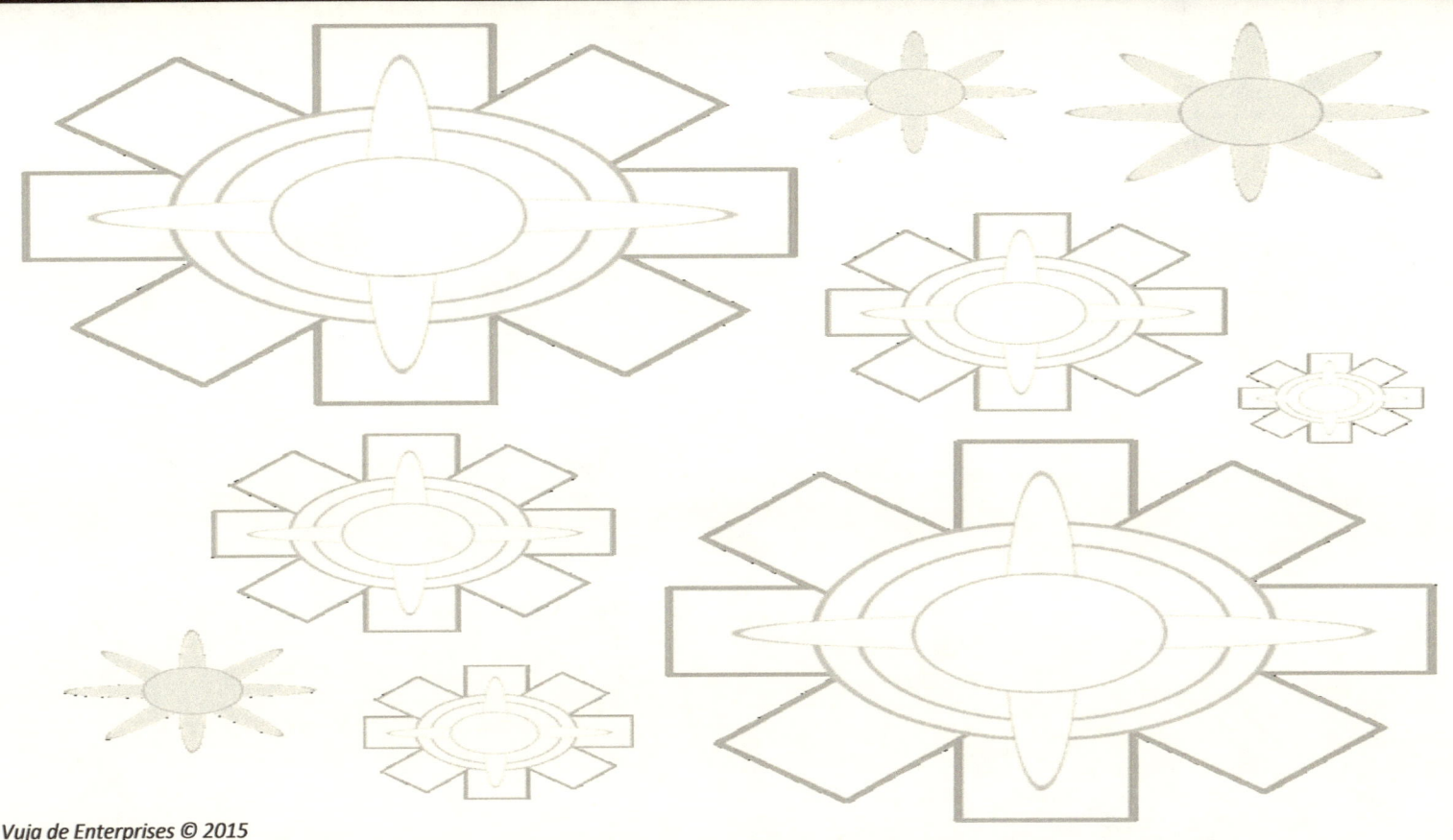

ZEN SHAPES #9

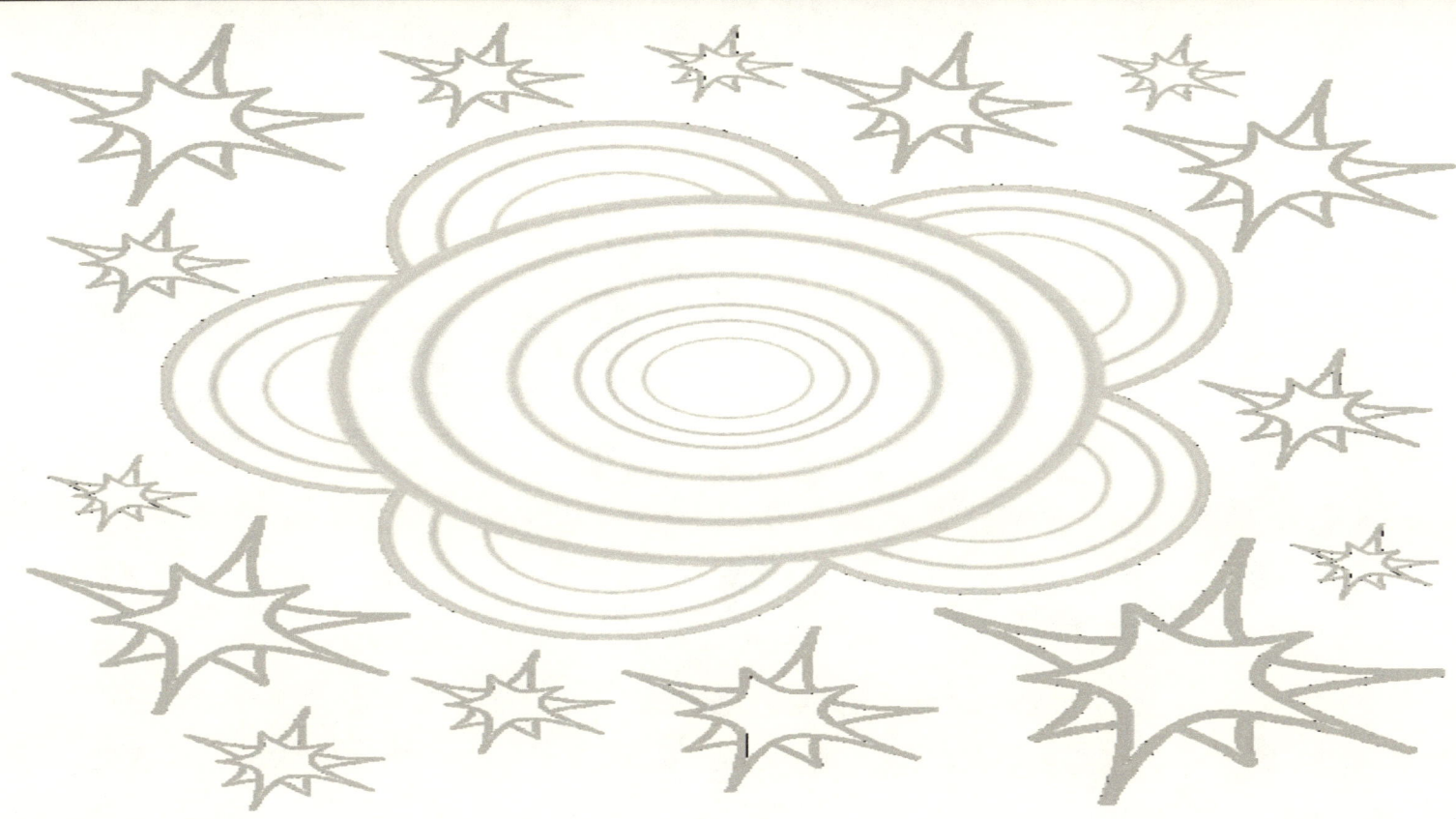

ZEN SHAPES #10

DIRECTIONS: Fill in each shape with a different design. Use shapes, lines, colors, and words to be as creative as you can! As you draw, think about how each shape connects with the shapes next to it – and seek to create a cohesive and unique design that speaks to your soul.

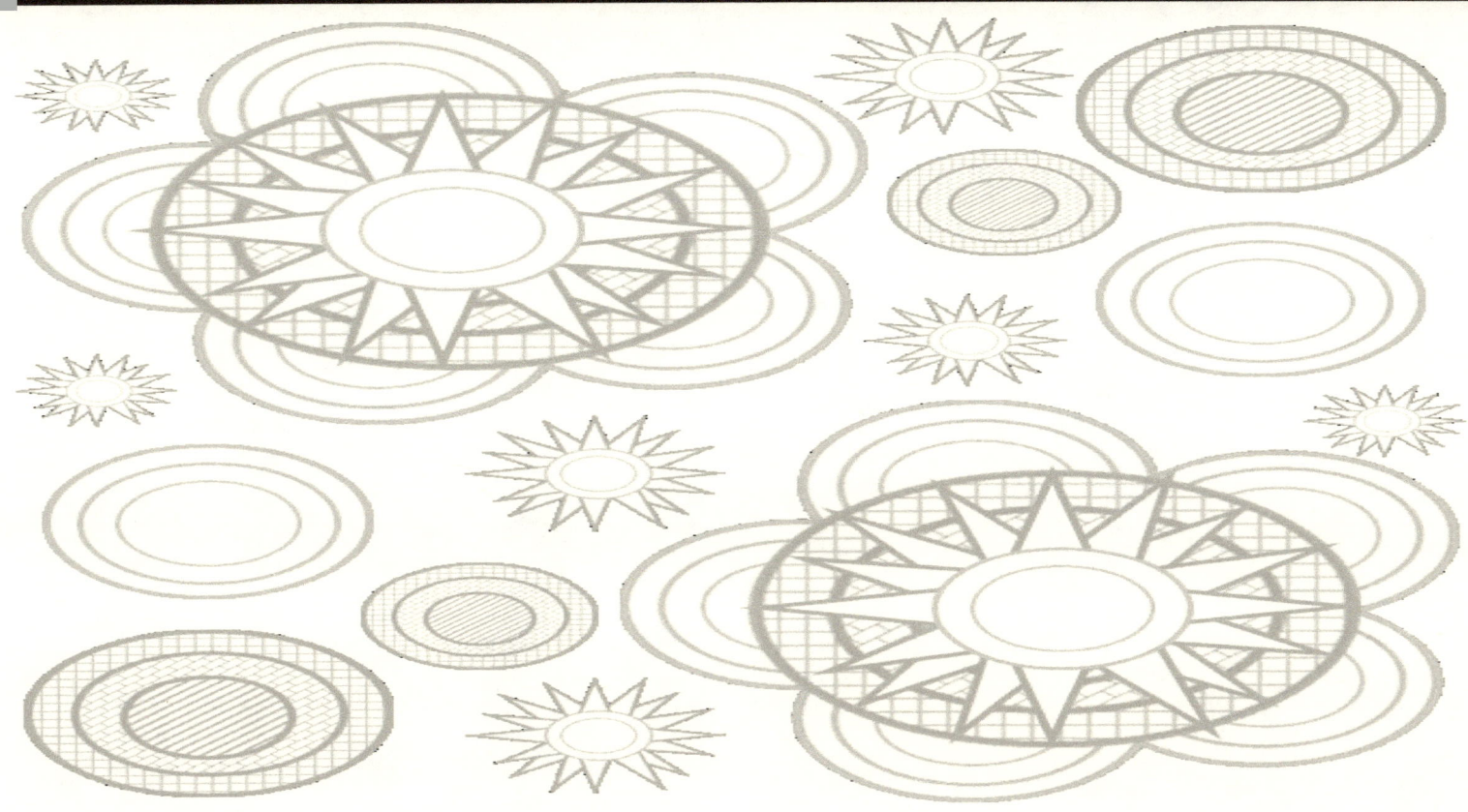

ZEN SHAPES #11

DIRECTIONS: Fill in each shape with a different design. Use shapes, lines, colors, and words to be as creative as you can! As you draw, think about how each shape connects with the shapes next to it – and seek to create a cohesive and unique design that speaks to your soul.

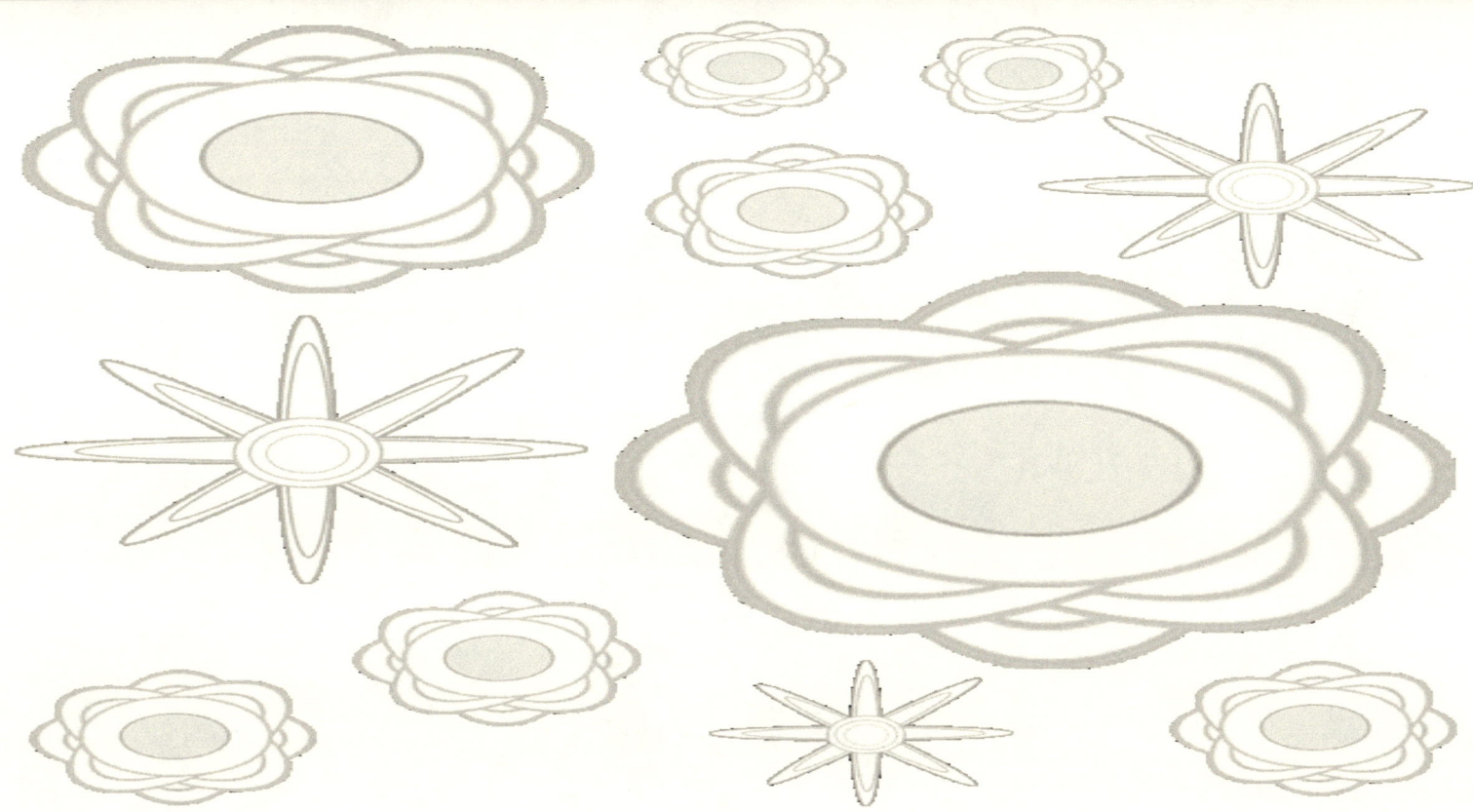

ZEN SHAPES #12

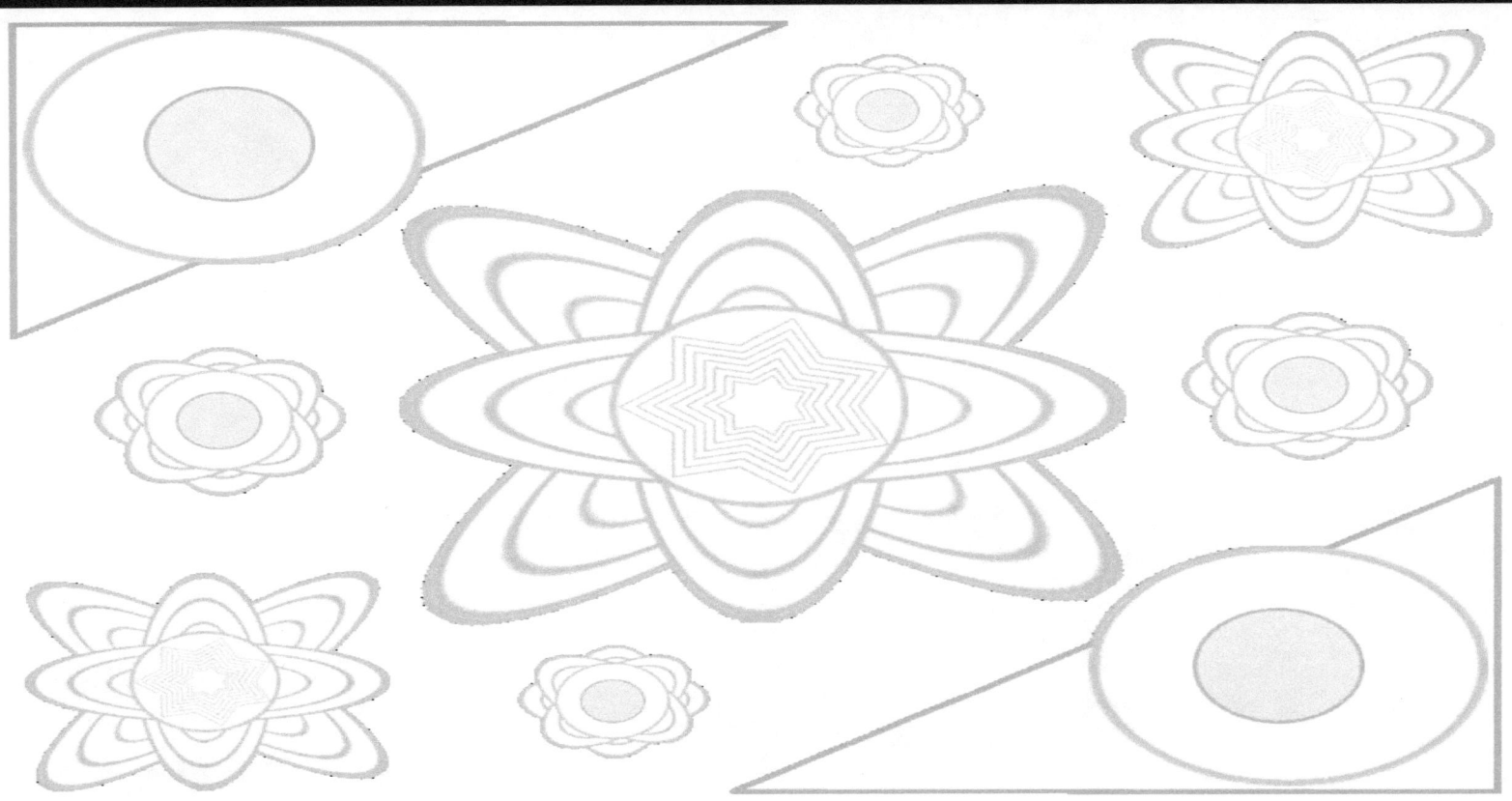

ZEN SHAPES #13

DIRECTIONS: Fill in each shape with patterns, designs, shapes, colors, and words to be as creative as you can! As you draw, think about how each shape connects with the shapes next to it – and seek to create a cohesive and unique design that speaks to your soul.

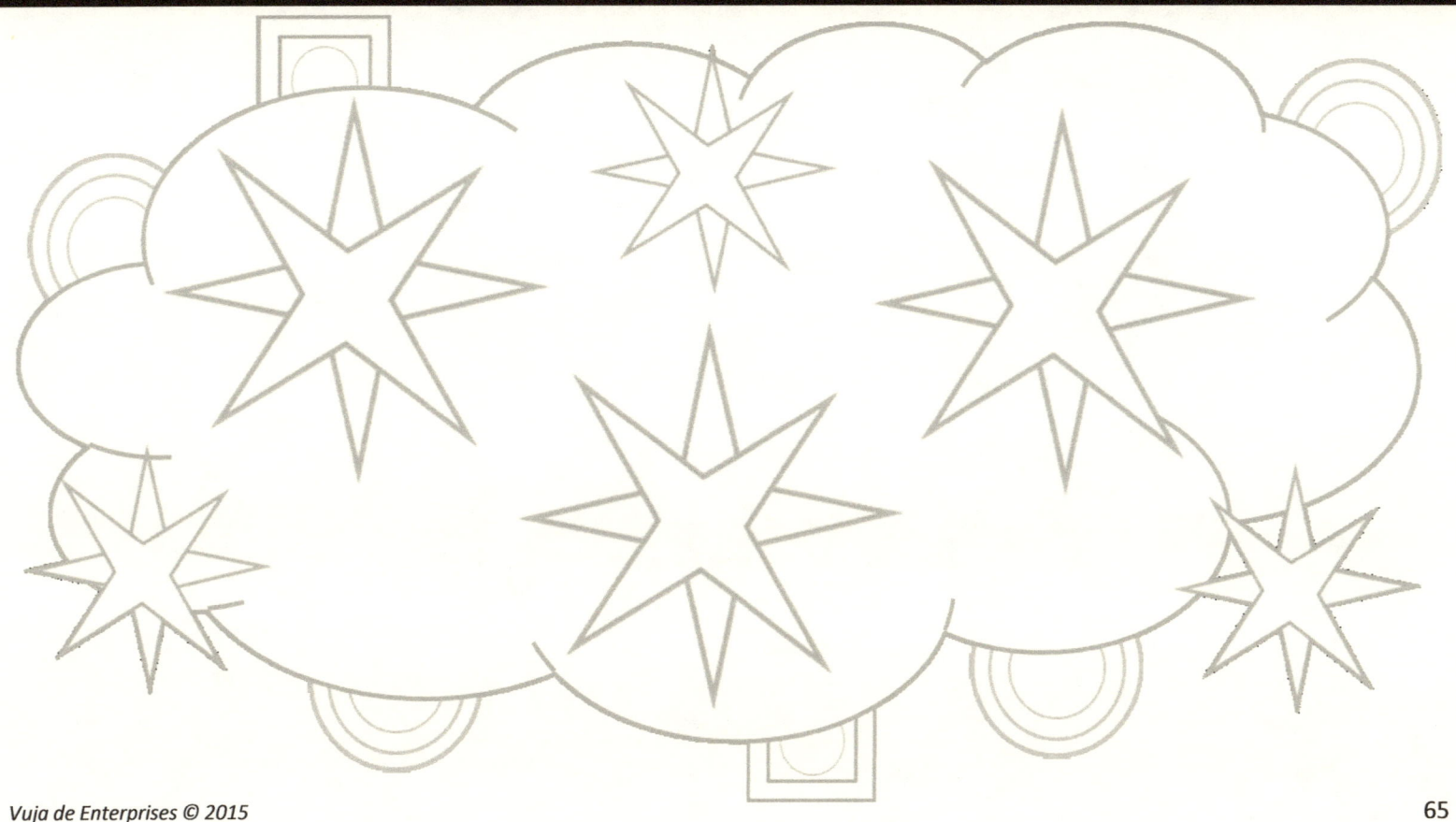

ZEN SHAPES #14

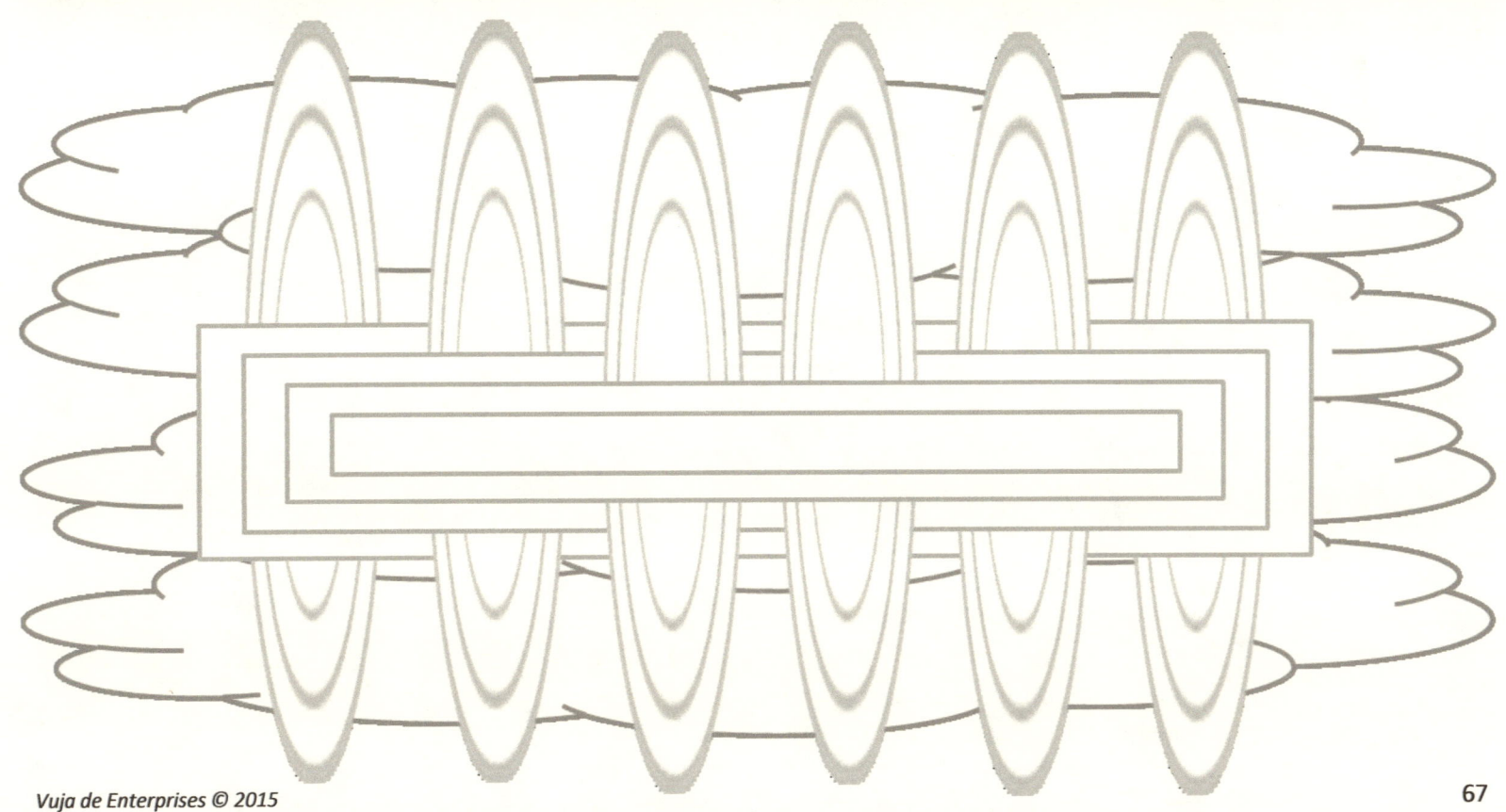

Vuja de Enterprises © 2015

ZEN SHAPES #15

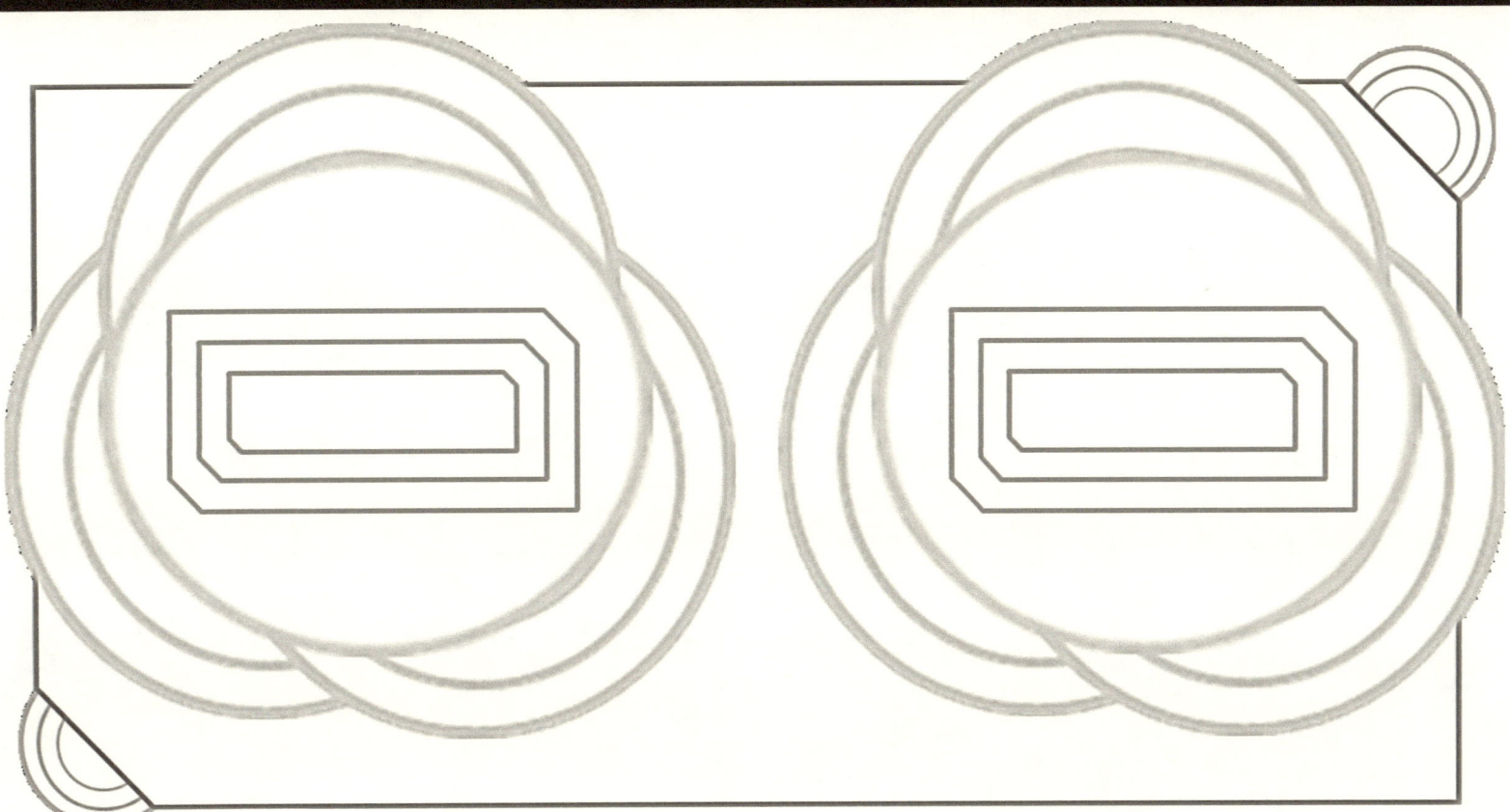

ZEN

COLORING PAGES FOR ADULTS

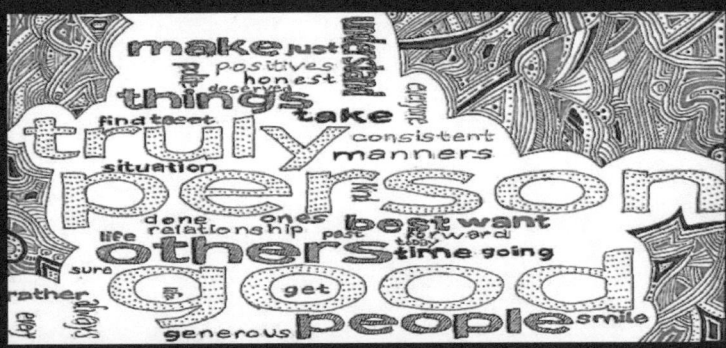
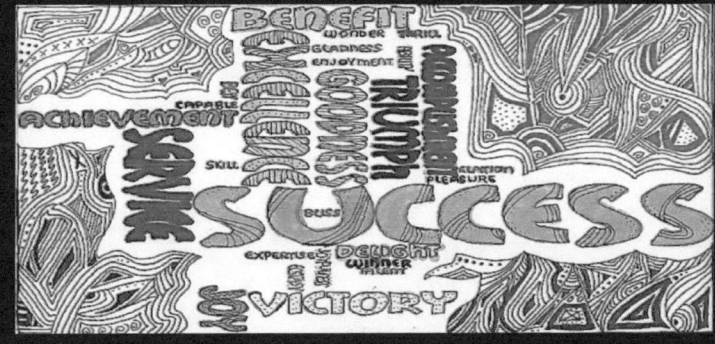

WORDLES

WORDLES #1

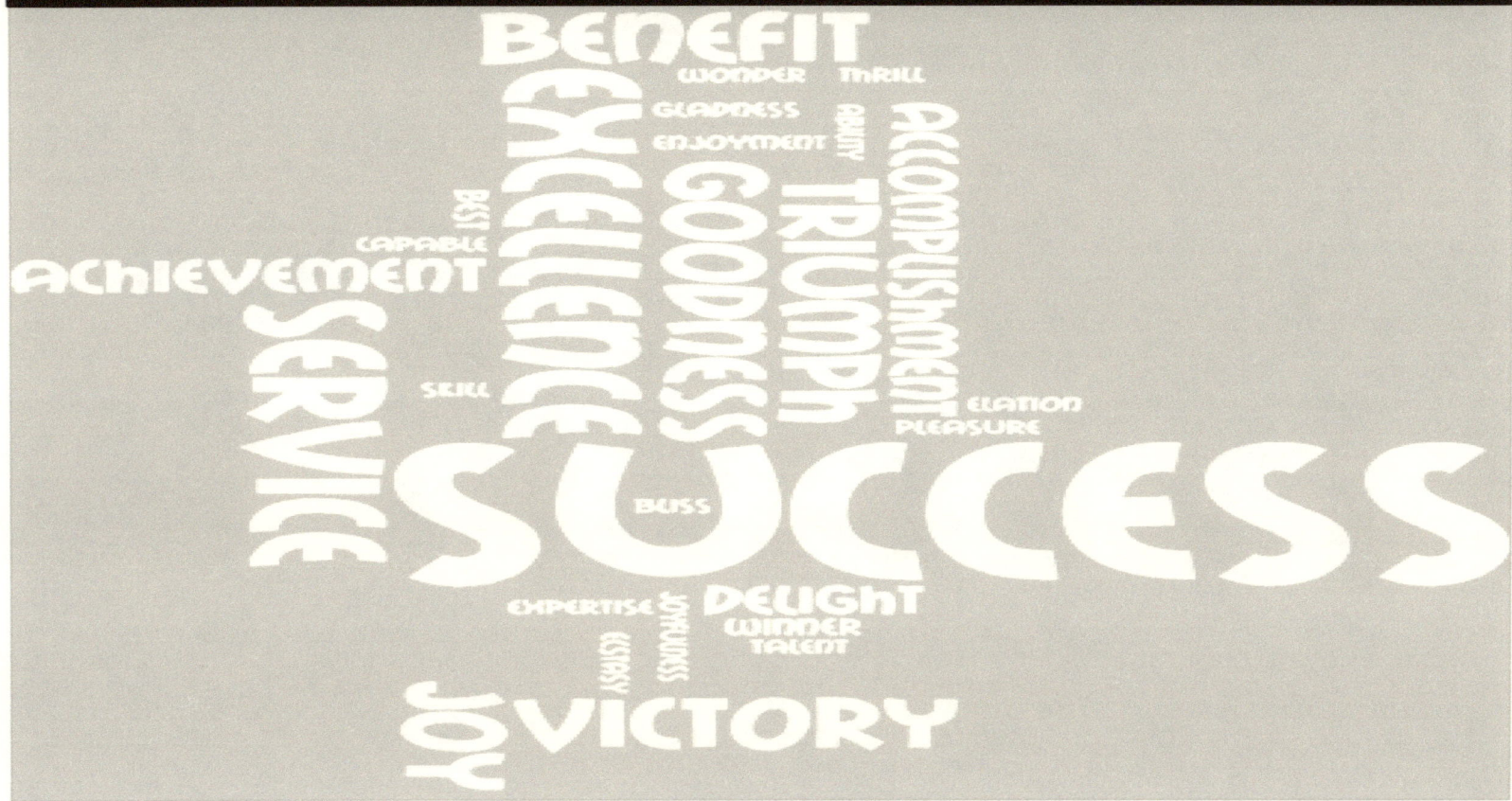

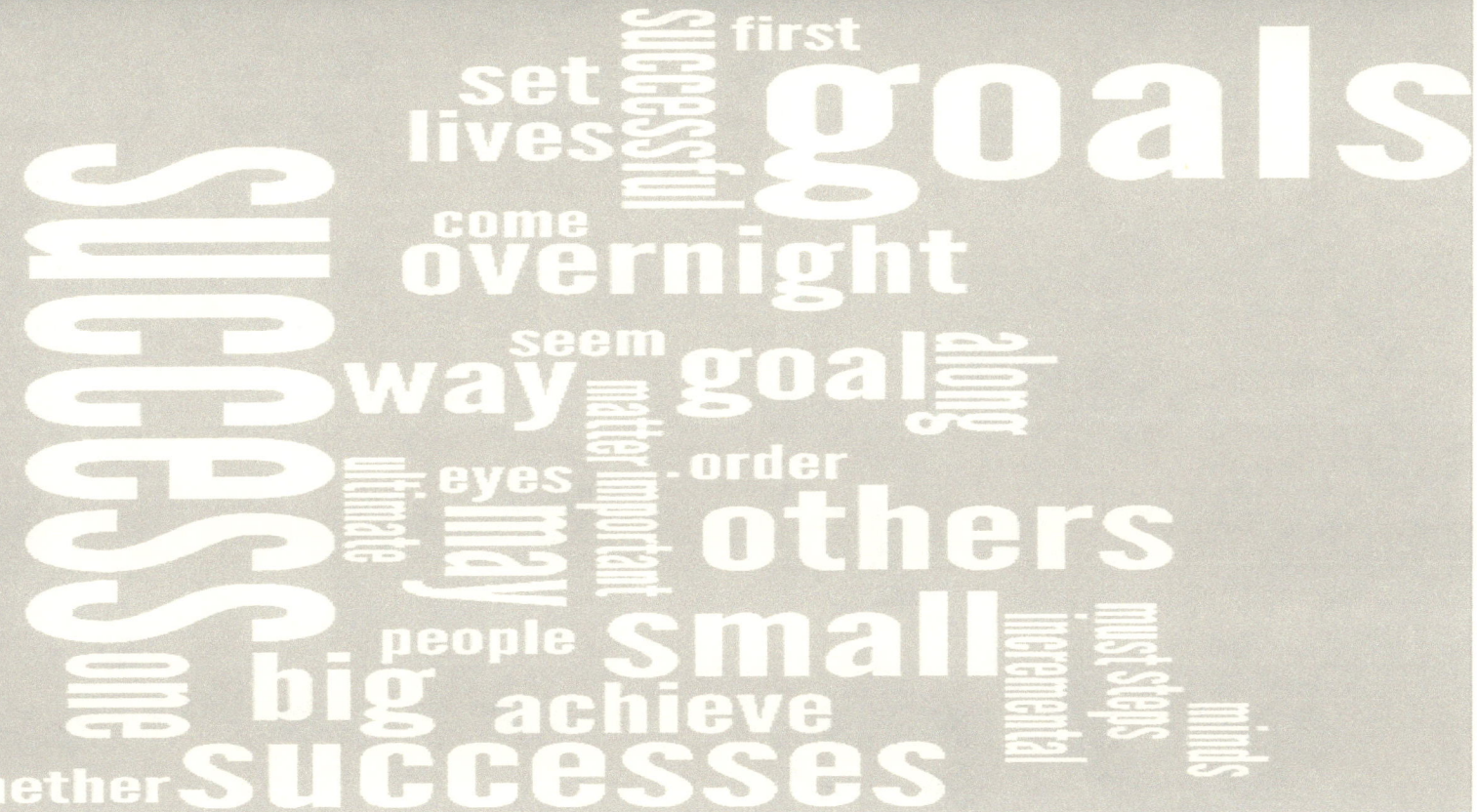

DIRECTIONS: Fill in each word with a different design. Use shapes, lines, and colors to be as creative as you can! As you draw, think about how each word connects with the words next to it – and seek to create a cohesive and unique design that speaks to your soul.

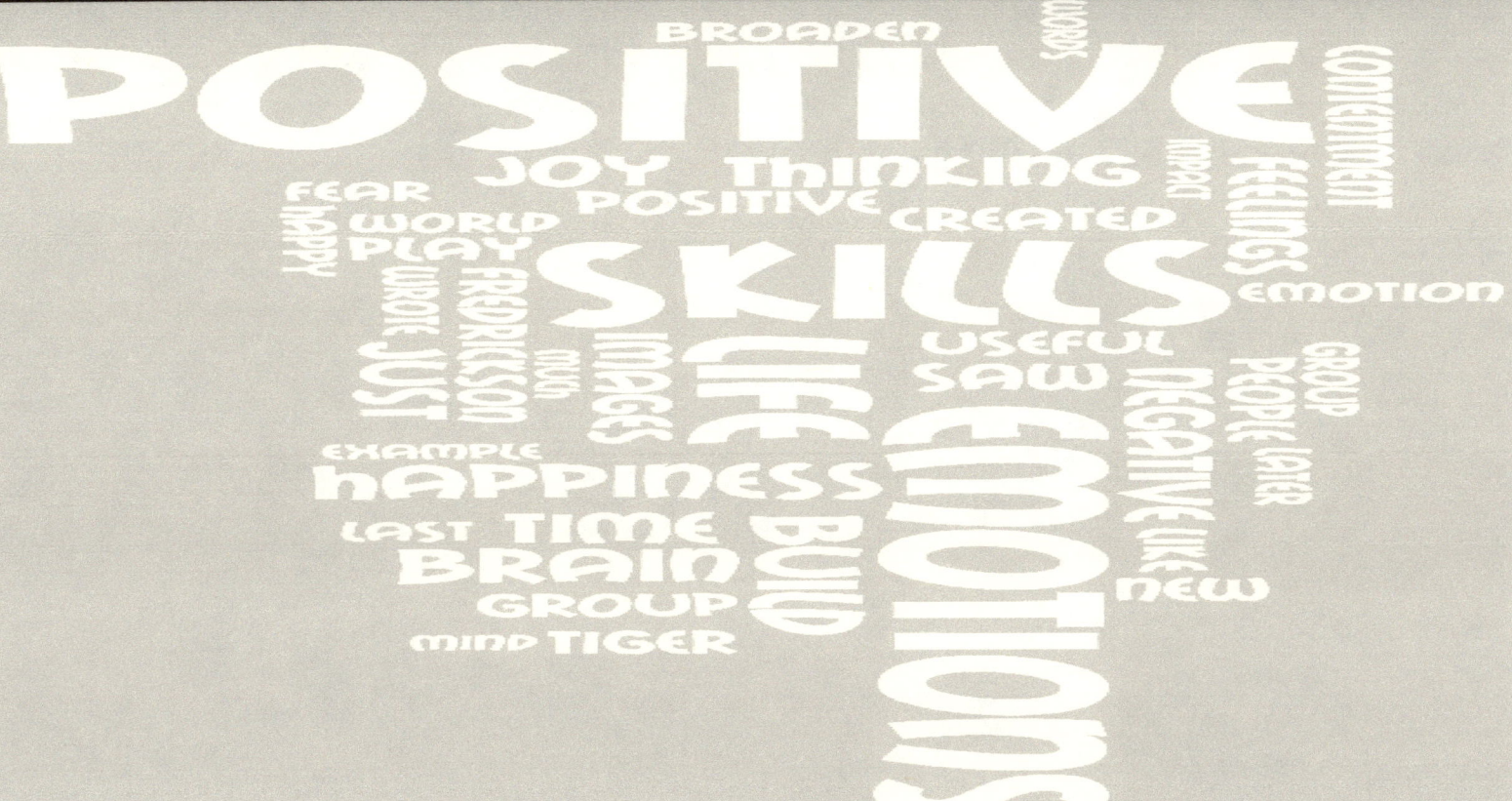

WORDLES #4

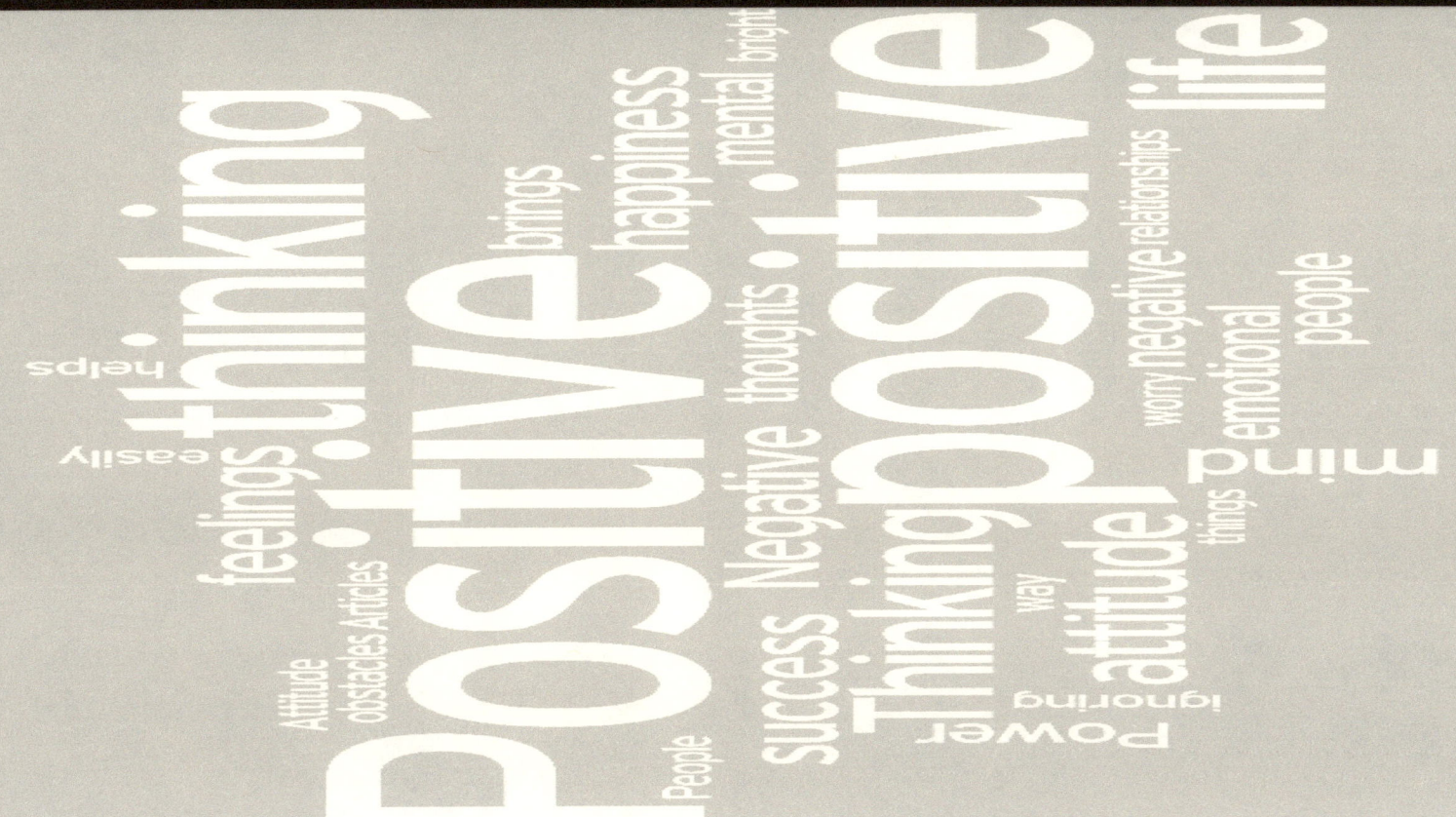

WORDLES #5

DIRECTIONS: Fill in each word with a different design. Use shapes, lines, and colors to be as creative as you can! As you draw, think about how each word connects with the words next to it – and seek to create a cohesive and unique design that speaks to your soul.

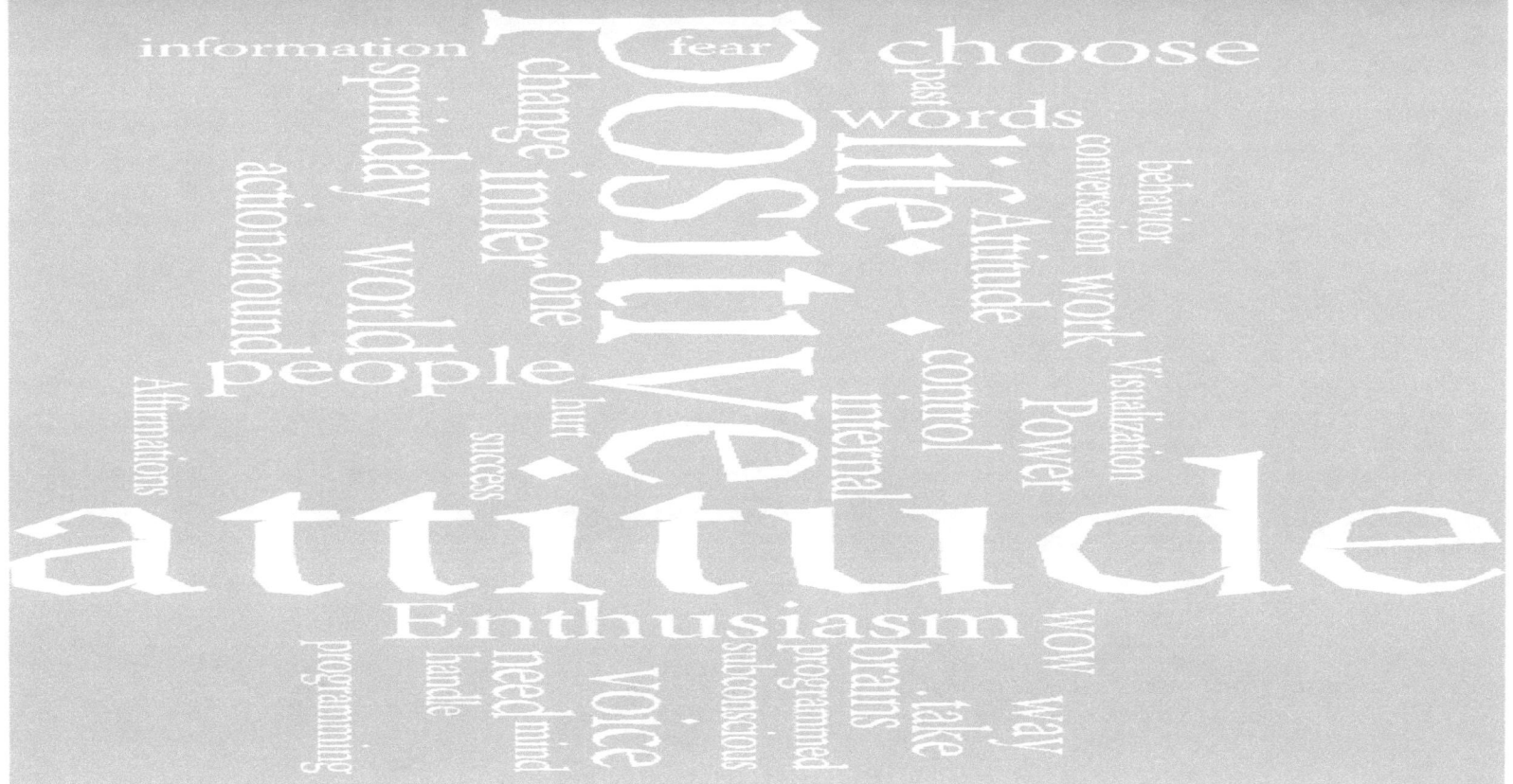

WORDLES #6

THINGS SOMEONE MAY EVEN
CHANGE FEEL LET BECOME
NEVER OTHERS
ISSUES
ONE MAY GOING EMOTIONS ALSO LIVE
NEED PEACE
ELSE EXAMPLE TIME INNER JUST
LIKE FEAR WORK
REALLY EVERY SITUATION MIND DAY LIFE AWARE
WILLING TOWARDS MAKE KNOW
THINK GO

DIRECTIONS: Fill in each word with a different design. Use shapes, lines, and colors to be as creative as you can! As you draw, think about how each word connects with the words next to it – and seek to create a cohesive and unique design that speaks to your soul.

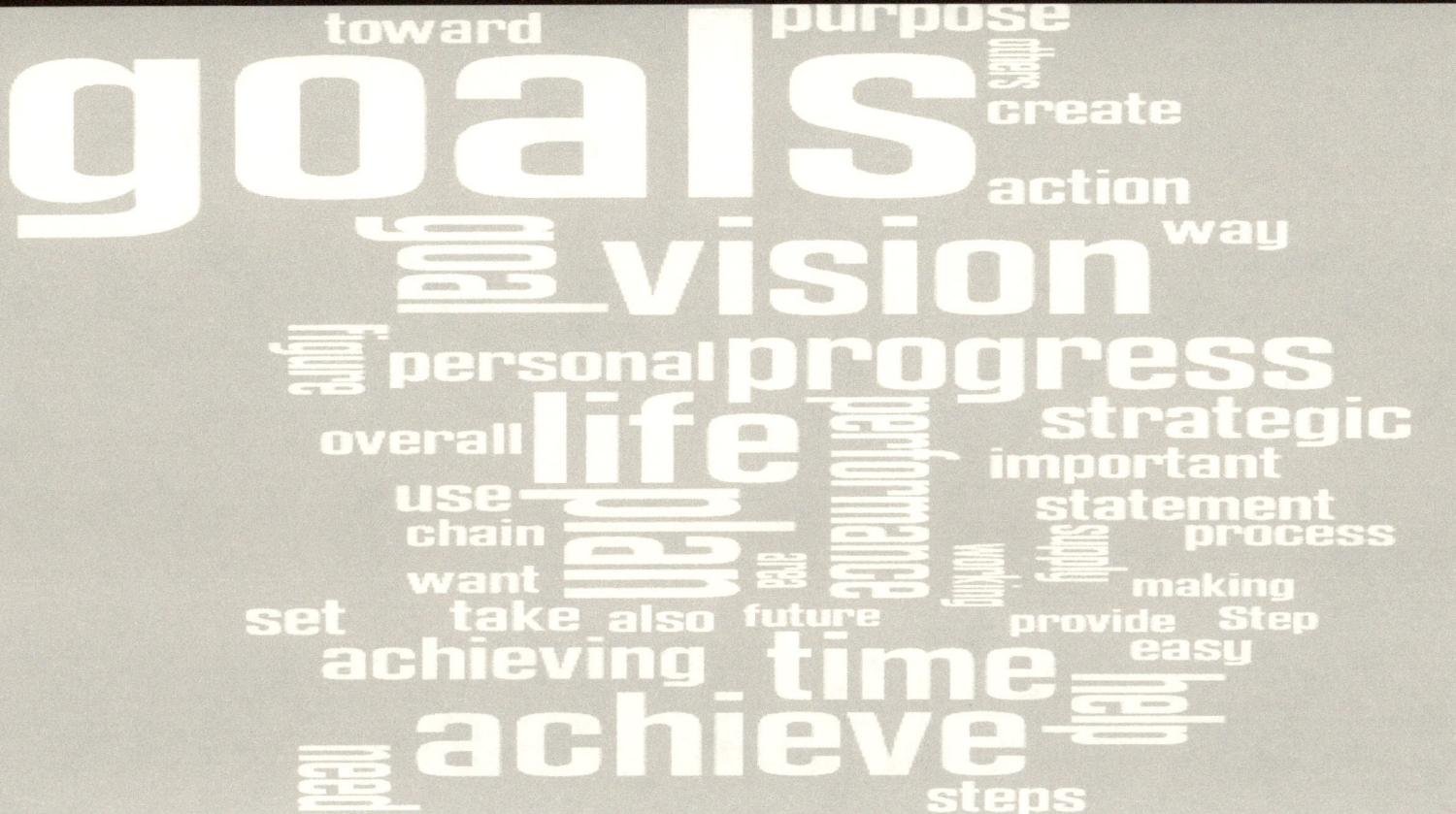

WORDLES #8

FOCUS
SURE
ADD
ACCOMPLISH
END
GOALS
HAPPEN SUCCESS KNOW
GOAL MAKE
GOAL
DEFINED
TIME ONE WANT
PERSONAL
PLAN PERCENT
MOTIVATING
SET GOALS STEPS
WORK
EXPENSES GET
WAY TIP
IMPORTANT
SMART SETTING
MAKE
DIRECTION REDUCE
USE
SET ACTUALLY
ACHIEVED
MUST

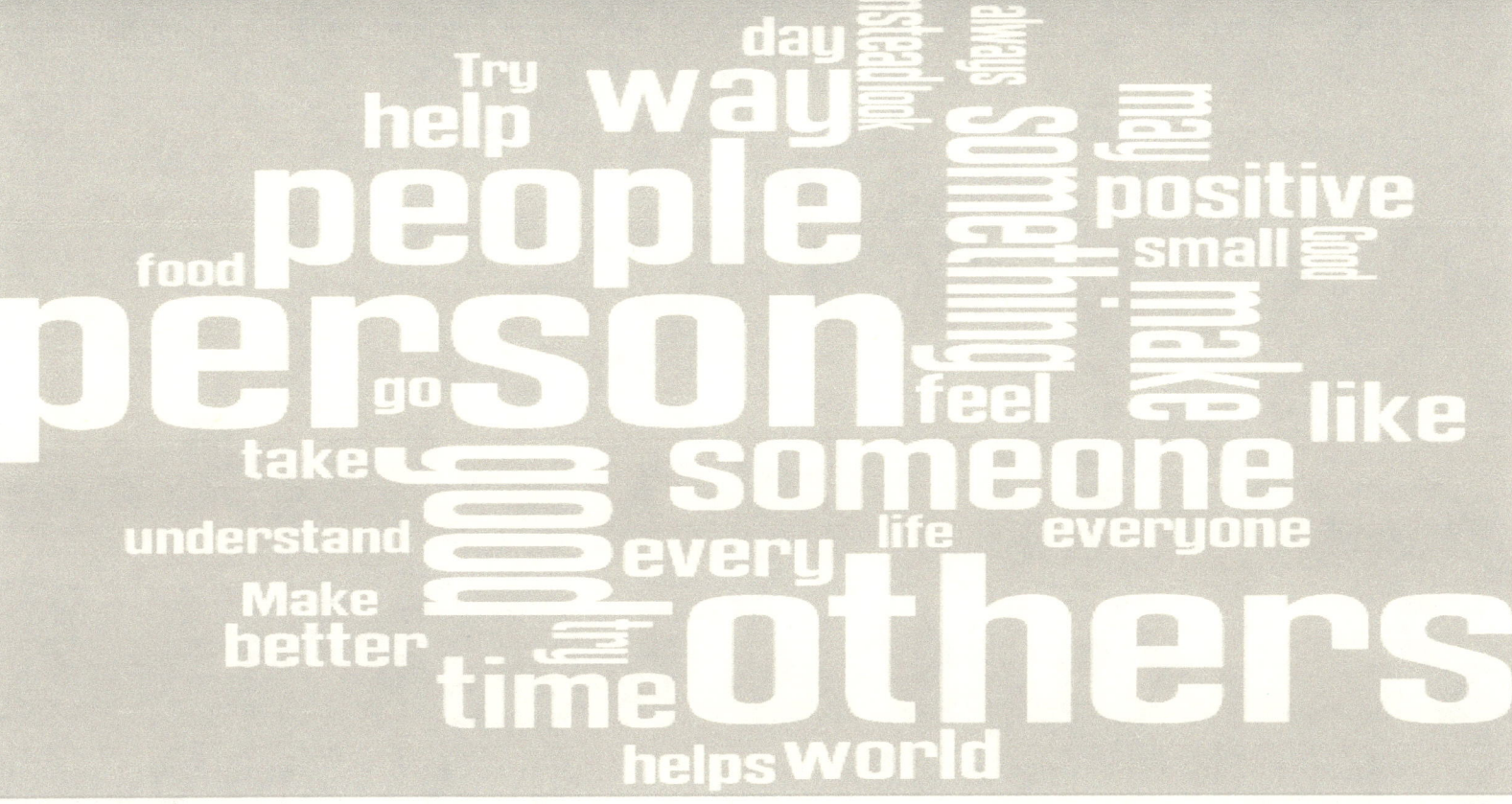

DIRECTIONS: Fill in each word with a different design. Use shapes, lines, and colors to be as creative as you can! As you draw, think about how each word connects with the words next to it – and seek to create a cohesive and unique design that speaks to your soul.

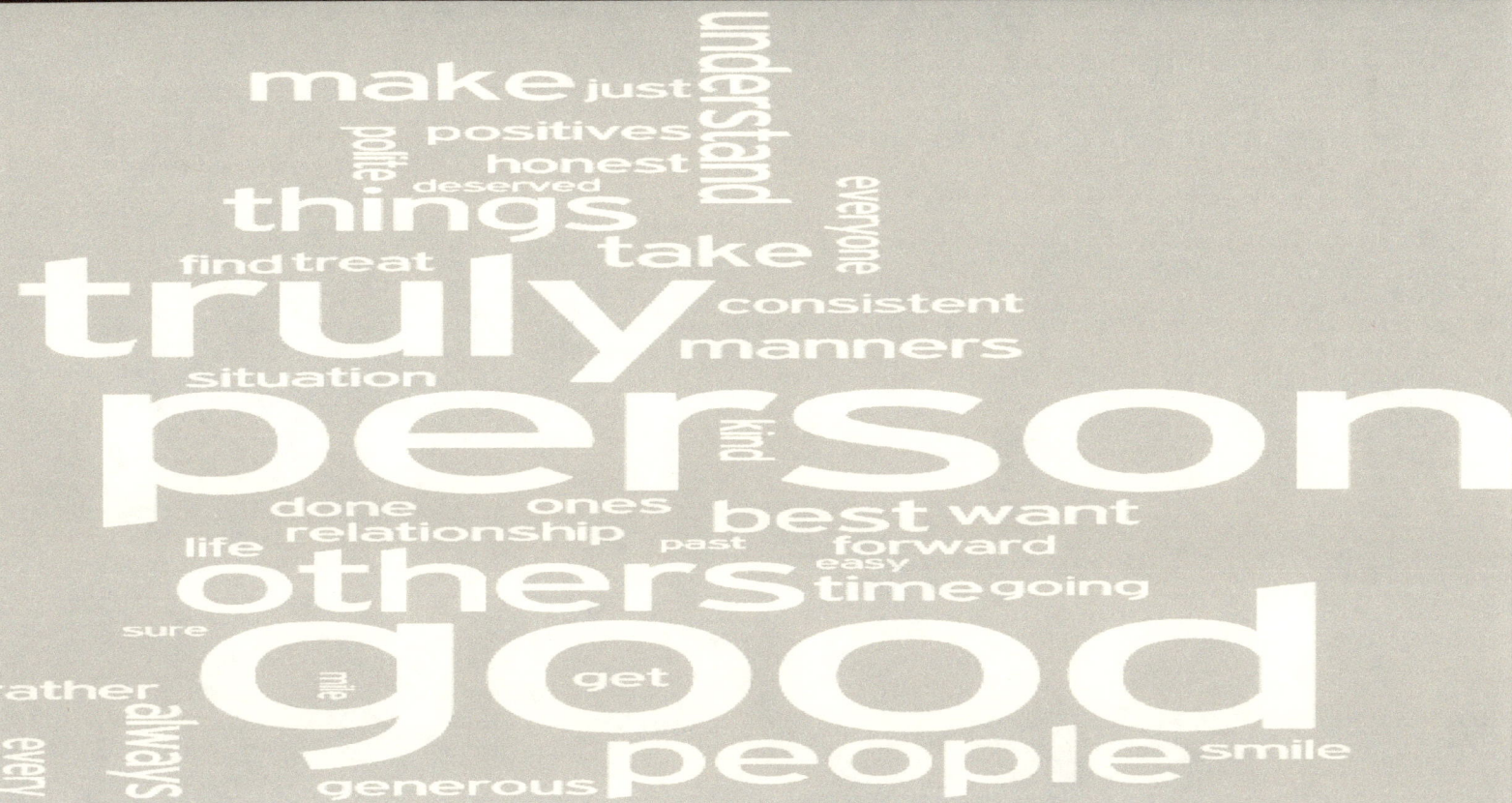

Learn
think people
values
good authentic
story just
make imposed
less rules month
Make get
assets value
others things income
person believe feel
improve
someone parents
new day gifts
excellence
want one
time life always
act every
something lucky
vision

DIRECTIONS: Fill in each word with a different design. Use shapes, lines, and colors to be as creative as you can! As you draw, think about how each word connects with the words next to it – and seek to create a cohesive and unique design that speaks to your soul.

get
time
live new work items
something right
one goals
trying
may life living
know list recognize
well always also
make
problem better things
priorities going
important approach
likelearning
recovery
daily take today
learn
day just
worry
muchneed

DIRECTIONS: Fill in each word with a different design. Use shapes, lines, and colors to be as creative as you can! As you draw, think about how each word connects with the words next to it – and seek to create a cohesive and unique design that speaks to your soul.

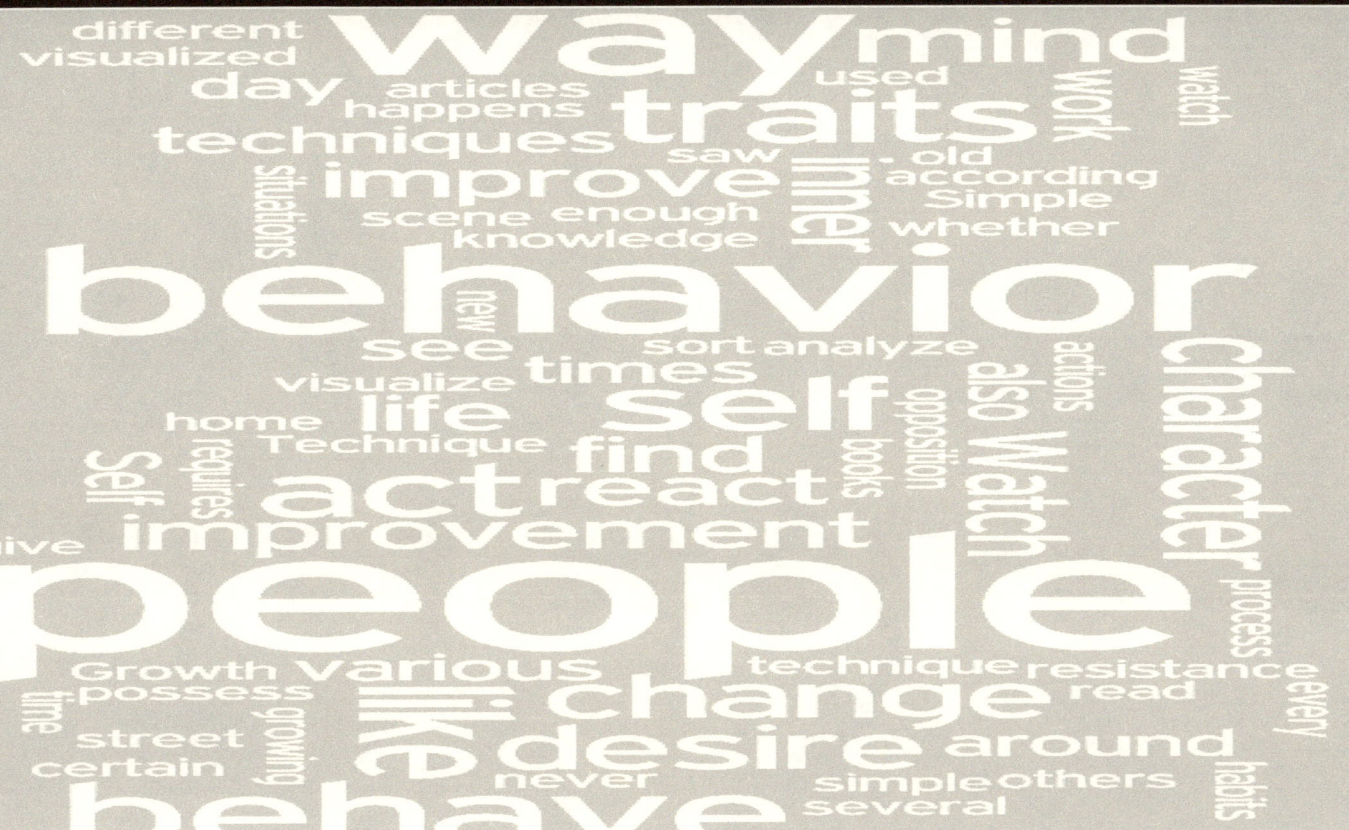

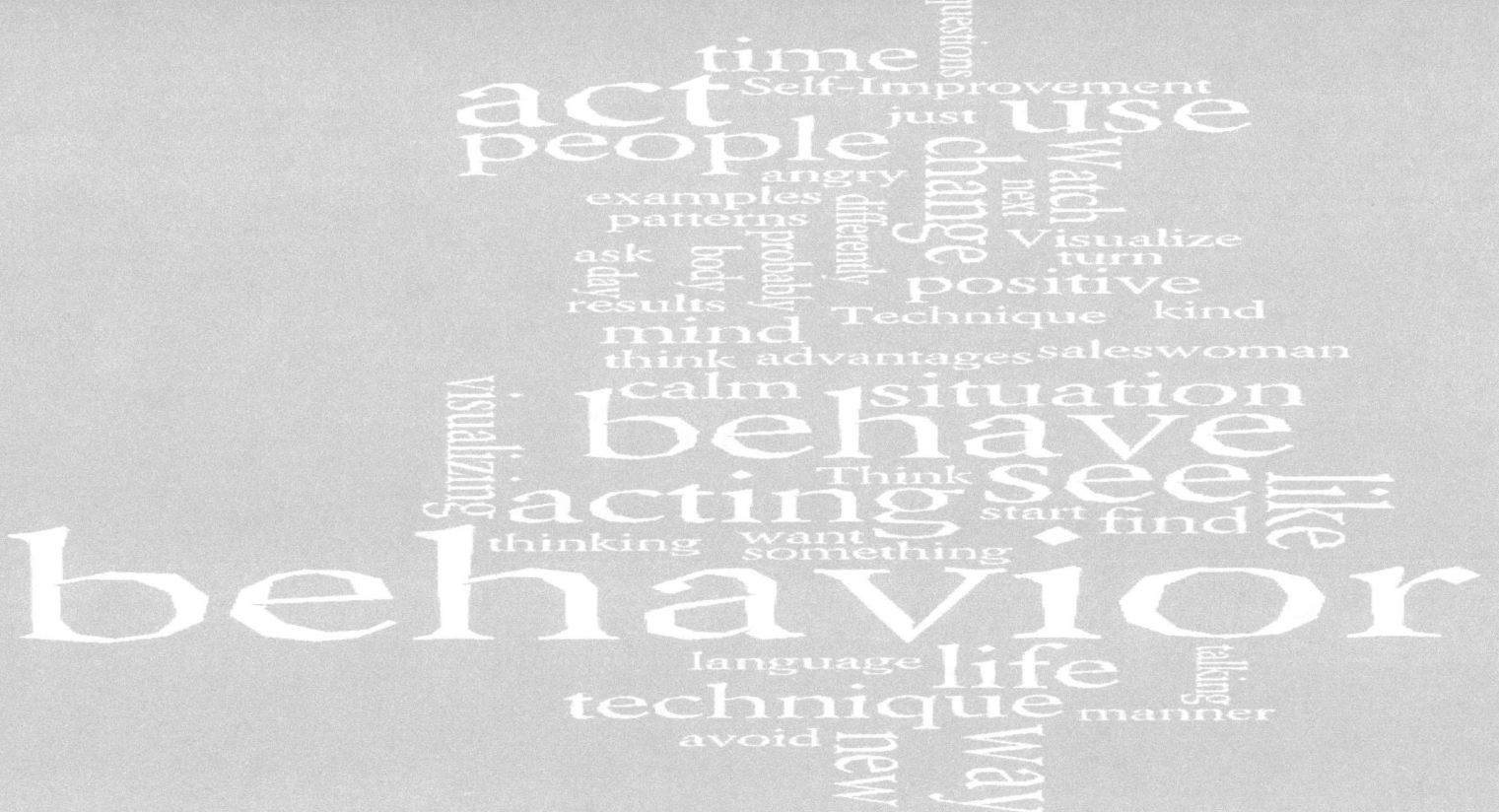

DIRECTIONS: Fill in each word with a different design. Use shapes, lines, and colors to be as creative as you can! As you draw, think about how each word connects with the words next to it – and seek to create a cohesive and unique design that speaks to your soul.

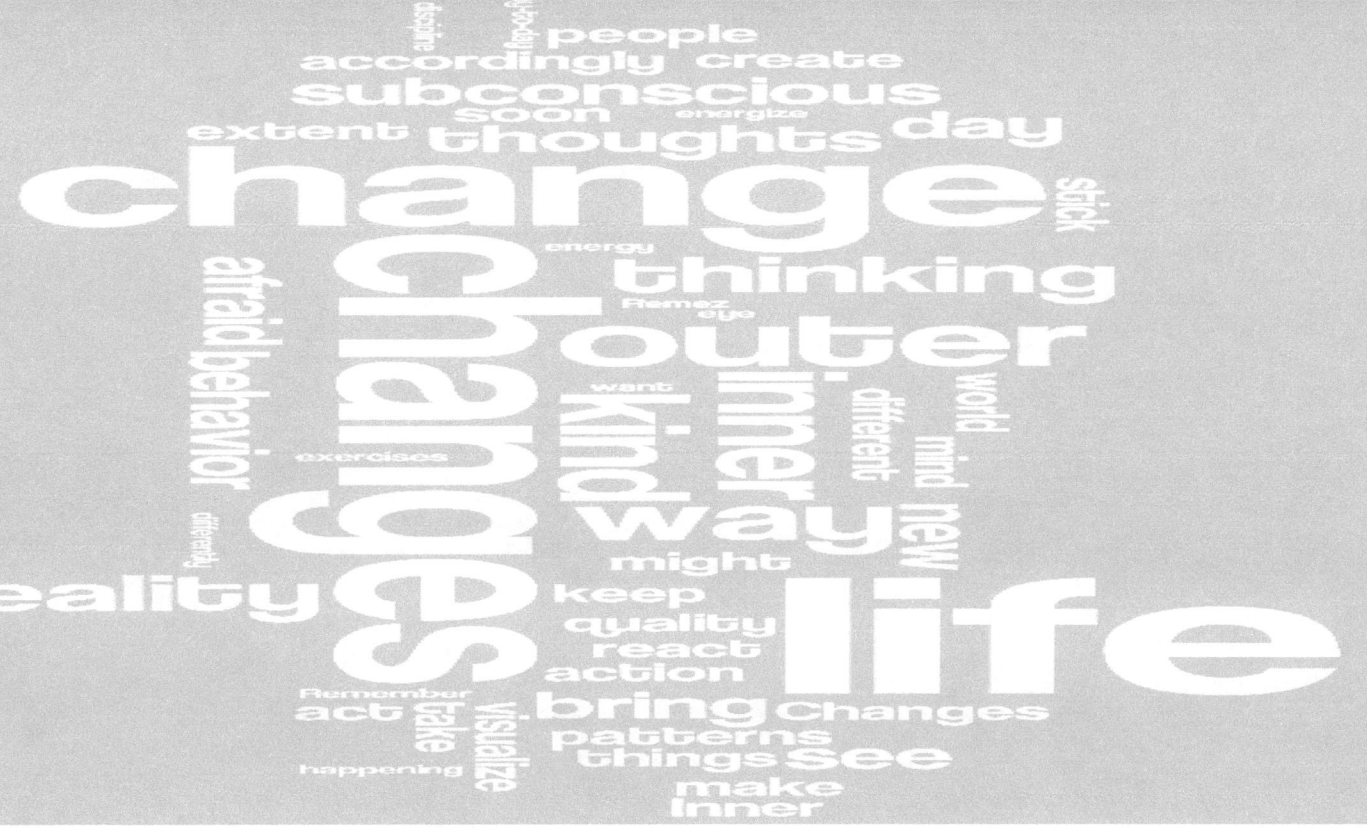